A Mainstream Journalist's Report
on Interplanetary Diplomacy

The Challenge of Contact

by

Phillip H. Krapf

Origin Press
Novato, CA

Origin Press

1122 Grant Ave., Suite C, Novato, CA 94945
888.267.4446

OriginPress.com

Get updates and join the author's email list at:
TheChallengeofContact.com

© 2001 Phillip H. Krapf
Cover & interior design: Phillip Dizick

All rights reserved. No part of this book may be reproduced by any means or in any form whatsoever without written permission from the publisher, except for brief quotations embodied in literary articles or reviews.

Publisher's Cataloging-in-Publication
(Provided by Quality Books, Inc.)

Krapf, Phillip H.
    The challenge of contact : a mainstream journalist's report on interplanetary diplomacy / Phillip H. Krapf. —1st ed.
    p. cm.
    LCCN: 2001088560
    ISBN: 1-57983-008-0

    1. Human-alien encounters. 2. Unidentified flying objects   I. Title.

BF2050.K73 2001   001.942
                          QBI01-700493

Printed in the United States of America
10 9 8 7 6 5 4 3 2 1

Dedication

This book is dedicated to the pioneers, the thousands—I don't know if anyone really knows the magnitude—who have gone before me, from a time stretching back decades at least, and perhaps centuries.

No one who has not had an experience can fully appreciate how profoundly it touches the very core of one's existence. And yet the reactions to such an event are as diverse as the individual members of the species itself, from tranquil acceptance to an energized quest for understanding. Some have been traumatized while others have been inspired. There is deep confusion and enlightenment. There is anger, elation, serenity, puzzlement, and fear. Some have been intellectually stimulated while others harbor worrisome doubts. Some have had their faith in humanity and hope for the future renewed. Others are conflicted.

Some have been eager and willing to speak about their adventure while others clutch it to their breasts like a dark secret.

**Someday,
we will all understand.**

Contents

Acknowledgements vi
Foreword vii
Preface xv
Recap of My Initial Contact xix
The Summit Timetable xxv

part 1

1. A Walk in the Park 1
2. Surprise Visitor 23
3. Reunion 35
4. Serious Business 57
5. The Metaphysical Universe 71
6. Revelations 93
7. The Probe 109
8. The Grilling 118
   Epilogue 137
   APPENDIX:
   .Verdant Lifespans and Time Measurement . . 140

part 2

Reporter's Notebook 142
The News Business and the ET Presence . . . 170

Acknowledgements

Timothy Wyllie appeared in my life at a critical moment, almost like—well, an angel. He came out of nowhere, a stranger, and with no solicitation on my part he assumed the task of clearing the path for this manuscript, shepherding it to the right place, the right people, at the right time. His selfless effort saved me literally months of time and labor, for which I am genuinely grateful.

Timothy is a bestselling author, and one of his books, *Dolphins, ETs and Angels*, is popularly considered a classic in the field.

Because he disappeared from my life as mysteriously as he appeared, I shall use this venue to say, "Thanks, Timothy, it has been an honor and a pleasure."

Byron Belitsos, publisher and CEO of Origin Press, patiently and diligently labored long hours for many months to bring this project to fruition. His business savvy, professional expertise and personal guidance were invaluable contributions from start to finish. His immersion of self into this work transcended the normal call of duty and became what surely must be described as a labor of devotion.

Matthew Gilbert was given the arduous task of taking a rather unwieldy manuscript to edit and restructure into a cohesive and readable form. He steered a true and clear course that has earned him my respect as one editor to another.

Naturally, all errors of fact and language that may have crept into the final product—as well as omissions, oversights and any other nasty little gremlins that are always on the prowl to cause mischief—are mine and mine alone.

Foreword

In *The Challenge of Contact* Phillip Krapf asks us to believe in many exotic and paradigm-evolving notions all at once. Many are so exotic as to stretch even my very open-minded vision of what's possible. For example, this book asks us to believe that at least some UFOs are real extraterrestrial spacecraft; that at this moment a large craft called the *Goodwill* is hovering behind Earth's moon; that since 1997 hundreds of prominent humans have been on this ship and are engaged in a kind of intergalactic diplomacy; and that these benevolent beings from afar are proposing a summit with representatives of Earth—indeed, Krapf claims that we are about to take an unimaginably beautiful step, as we begin preparations to meet a race of highly advanced and peace-loving beings from a planet many light-years away, and are soon to be inducted into an interplanetary federation a la Star Trek. On top of all this, Krapf's book also asks us to believe in angels and to consider the plausibility of reincarnation.

Is *The Challenge of Contact* simply an interesting work of fiction posing as fact? I've talked to Phillip twice on the phone as part of my regular process of inquiring about unusual books I come across. His first book, *The Contact Has Begun*, deserved a call a couple of years ago to get at least a gut check on the man. He seemed then—as now—like a gentle, honest person. He doesn't write like he's lying; his account appears to come from the heart. One would think that a retired editor with the *L.A. Times* who shared a Pulitzer Prize could do a much better job of constructing and penning such a story if he were trying to make a bestseller out of it.

This book requires suspended judgment in a number of ways. Phillip Krapf doesn't need to be lying to be just plain wrong. He could simply be self-deceived, which, to his credit, he does not absolutely rule out. I could therefore dismiss these wonderings and conclude that *The Challenge of Contact* is another of the many hallucinations of our richly textured consciousness. Or, I could dismiss it as some sort of mental manipulation by unknown forces. Or, let's say he really is deceiving us and that this book, as well as his last book, are nothing more than a joke being perpetrated on the UFO community by debunkers in order to see who they might snare.

Who knows what happened to Phillip Krapf? I don't know.

But here's what I do believe to be true:

I believe that any of the major theories of physics now emerging into vogue could allow for such wonders as extraterrestrial travel. These include multidimensional string theory, stochastic electrodynamics theory, and recently re-emergent ether theories. As of May 2001, mainstream thinkers still haven't woken up to the implications of the latest and best theoretical work. These theories would help us understand phenomena well beyond the limits of the paradigm of physics established in the early decades of the 20th century. But since most mainstream media and science are still caught within the limits of this understanding of physics, contentions about interstellar travel and teleportation will be considered by most reporters and scientists as more than slightly nutty. But then, UFO research may also herald the day when these same defenders of the status quo will be seen as dogmatic or obstructionist. That's the day when the evidence for an ET presence may be more clearly evident, and when newer theories are fully promulgated among physicists.

For example, one concept arising from one of the simpler theories—stochastic electrodynamics—allows a reinterpretation of relativity theory that makes it plausible that one day soon we will construct spacecraft capable of travelling between stars as conveniently as we fly between continents. And if such wonders are in the future of human science, then it stands to reason that other civilizations across the universe have likely been traveling the grandest of all seas for longer than we can imagine. And, if all this is so, should it be all that surpising if one of these advanced races is here to monitor our activities and to ensure that we do not bring weapons into space once we construct such spacecraft?

I believe that the simplest explanations for a small percentage of the countless unidentifiable objects witnessed over many thousands of years of recorded human history involve spacecraft of extraterrestrial origin. In this connection, it has long been speculated that the United States government became aware of the reality of extraterrestrial visitation in the 1940s or 1950s at the latest, and that very tightly compartmentalized teams have been studying related exotic phenomena for decades. It has been advanced by many UFO researchers that the decision was made to conceal the UFO reality from the public for several reasons: a severe lack of information about extraterrestrial intentions, a good case of technological shock, and the transformative implications for the future of humanity. This logic becomes easier to grasp in the face of the exigencies of Cold War geopolitics.

In recent times, rumors, leaked documents, and firsthand accounts pull the focus of this story out of the skies and into locked laboratories. This information suggests that one or more UFOs have crashed or were otherwise acquired by the United States government in the '40s or '50s, and that amazingly advanced technologies for propulsion and energy generation, and even biological specimens, await more extensive public disclosure and coverage by the mainstream press.

I have carefully studied some parts of the large body of evidence of these allegations, and have had the opportunity to discuss these questions with multiple, and in some cases very senior eyewitnesses whose backgrounds I have very carefully checked. Based on this research, I believe that a very small, very well-concealed cluster of public-private organizations are well aware of the reality of visitation from other worlds. I further believe that physical materials from extraterrestrial craft have been recovered and studied. To the extent that this is true, I recommend withholding judgment on the wisdom of the decision to conceal such findings and the manner of stewardship of this matter over these past decades. Let future historians be their judges. In the meantime, a cosmic measure of brotherhood and mutual understanding is called for.

All of my beliefs are, of course, subject to correction by evidence. I could be entirely wrong on every point. But the evidence seems to be piling up in favor of the views I'm advancing.

When confronted with such beliefs, one does more soul-searching than is otherwise typical. If you come to believe in such notions as I have, you'll likely refocus the lens you use to discern what's true and what matters. You begin thinking of the longer term, and you start to see the beauty of our Earth a bit more clearly, and appreciate the diversities of life more deeply.

And countless questions pop into mind:

If some "aerial anomaly" evidence is objectively real, then why haven't these things landed on the White House lawn?

Why hasn't SETI discovered radio signals?

What are the real limits of future propulsion technology?

If real, how would such powers change our lives and societies?

What would it be like to voyage to another world? Why would we go?

Further, what are other forms of life on other planets going to be like?

Does the double helix of biology represent a particularly special process within nature?

How much more than pure random chance is sentient life?

What does this say about the nature of God?

In the light of all this, might there be some underlying universal principle that can be glimpsed through both the lens of objective science and the subjective inner sense of spirituality?

There's more: Is there really some kind of "galactic federation," as Phillip Krapf reports?

What are the cultures of other sentient life forms like?

How would we humans educate ourselves to behave toward other garden-like worlds we would discover, if it were possible for you and me to sail among the stars?

And would we not also one day find ourselves waiting for other young species to awaken—like the so-called Verdants that Krapf says are observing us?

If there are answers to these questions, would our lack of complete self-discovery to date be sufficient grounds to explain the nondestructive distance that the ETs appear to be keeping? Could it be true that they are waiting for Earth to give birth to a cosmic humanity—or that they are even playing a role in fostering this transformation?

When people who claim to have experienced extraterrestrial phenomena offer glimpses across a spectrum of possibilities, such as I find in this book, such new ideas can expand our wonderings about such epic questions.

I was drawn to Phillip's first book, *The Contact Has Begun*, and this present book, because of several factors, the combination of which I'd not seen very often in the course my readings.

First, and apparently unfamiliar to Phillip (reassuringly so, I might add, with respect to his credibility), is the correlation between his report of a future city to be called *Genesis* that will be humanity's first gateway to the stars, with spiritual traditions that speak of a city one day coming into existence as the point of contact between Heaven and Earth. Such a city is envisioned as a focal point for humanity's engagement with a higher and eternal purpose. As Phillip describes *Genesis*, it will be the place where humans and extraterrestrial beings first meet in large numbers, and through which our first voyages to other worlds will commence. Perhaps each classroom within the educational complex will teach a different world's history book. Perhaps *Genesis* is where the first human starfleet will originate.

Second, Phillip unknowingly describes a contact scenario compatible with the scientific worldview postulated by the category of physics theory in which I have greatest confidence. Some speculations about alien visitation have more to do with time travel, space-time warps, wormholes, stargates touching eleven dimensions, or whatever. This story of contact speaks of none of that. It reports of beings, called Verdants, who are quite like us, but vastly more advanced biologically and technologically. As we are, they once were . . . as they are, we may become . . . and the gaps between species might be understood in everyday terms that don't require a Ph.D. in physics.

Their spacecraft are reported to function in such a manner that their inventors would have discovered ages ago how to reproduce the influence of gravity through technological means—something we're coming closer to doing today. The beings who are reported to sail in these craft appear to have powers of consciousness that some believe exist in a less developed form within human beings, including telepathic communication.

There are numerous reasons to be deeply skeptical about Krapf's assertions: Guardian angels? Folksy English phrases spoken by ETs? Devices that recall memories and print them out?

And even more questions remain: For example, why is Krapf's representation of ET contact so clearly anthropocentric? (The Verdants exhibit what we would consider to be fully human features. This picture is either a valid scientific basis for rejection of the scenario, or suggests that there might be deeper harmonies among hominid forms than we've realized.)

And why would an advanced race of beings choose Phillip Krapf to communicate their message? Who knows if they did? Will the other so-called human "Ambassadors" that he claims have also been aboard the *Goodwill* eventually go public and corroborate his story? Without definitive answers to these questions, one is forced to say that Phil may be crazy, lying, or whatever. Again, I just don't know.

But in the end, if his story turns out to be true, he might have been chosen for other qualities that I appreciate about Phillip's writing: It's simple, humble, ordinary, unpretentious, and uncolored by religious dogma.

One thing is certain: The future will surely answer all of these questions, including the question of whether Krapf's story is true.

For me, this book was an interesting read. And regardless of whether or not it turns out to reflect a cosmic reality, I'll repeat a firm belief: Human beings are awakening to the possibility that the generations alive today could become the extraterrestrials of *other* garden worlds. I believe it is our destiny to evolve into membership among peaceful and sublime galactic civilizations, voyaging among never-ending wonders, across an infinite sea of stars.

Whatever the future's scenario of contact may turn out to be, we may be approaching a new beginning—the most remarkable chapter yet written in the saga of Earth's young, promising, and hopeful family of sentient life.

—Joe Firmage
May 1, 2001

Preface

It is remarkably strange to be a mainstream journalist who has encountered extraterrestrial creatures—all the more so given that I was recruited to literally speak on behalf of an alien race called the Verdants, to act as their designated reporter regarding their ongoing agenda for contact with Earth that involves an extensive program of interplanetary diplomacy. This book continues my reporting on my latest contacts with the Verdants, and provides an update as of March 2001 on their unfolding plans for imminent contact with the peoples of Earth.

When I first went public with this story in *The Contact Has Begun* in 1998, many of my friends and most of my former colleagues at the *Los Angeles Times* began—not surprisingly—to distance themselves from me. Simultaneously, I came into contact with a whole new group of people, researchers into the UFO phenomenon who have remained quite out of the mainstream eye, in my estimation, for much too long. This relatively small community—many of whom strike me as credible, sincere, and courageous—grapples almost daily with a story of cosmic proportions. As the mainstream press stands by almost oblivious, a historic controversy now rages as to how to interpret the UFO/ET-abduction phenomenon. Arguably the most important issue of the last half century, perhaps of all time, still remains a largely underground phenomenon.

Among those who follow this story, there seems to be three or four schools of thought—usually at odds—on the reasons behind extraterrestrial contact. The first considers ETs to simply be ill intentioned, seeking to intervene in our

preface XV

affairs and our individual lives for their own benefit, without concern for the welfare of Earth or its peoples. The second group takes the opposite tack, contending that an organized federation of benign civilizations from other planets is here to share their more advanced technologies and ideas of peaceful living with a world that desperately needs them—when that world is ready. A third and smaller group adds another layer, pointing to the possibility of an extra-dimensional presence, wise angelic observers who are watching and waiting to see how events unfold—and providing celestial influence as the occasion requires. Finally there are those who give the whole affair a political spin, arguing that it's not the aliens we have to fear, but rogue elements in our own government, acting in concert with "deep black" figures in the military and private industry to manipulate the human population with advanced systems of mind control and manipulation—perhaps even deploying ET technologies that have been captured—and motivated by some sinister human agenda.

Naturally, I have been inundated by all sorts of theories, postulations, conjectures and so on regarding what "really" happened in the case of my abduction by the Verdants in 1997. Many of those who have written me, including established UFO researchers, have offered a variety of interpretations for my experience, unwilling to accept at face value the way I have described it. I'll admit that I have not closed my mind completely to some of these alternative explanations. But until someone can convince me otherwise, I must continue to believe what my sensory impressions tell me—that my encounters were real and happened in the way I remembered and reported on them in my first book.

Nevertheless, I have been tireless in trying to retain my objectivity. After all, being a natural skeptic, and a career news reporter and editor, I believe I have an open mind, and I still at times consider the possibility that others are right and I am wrong about the nature of my experience, that perhaps I was duped by unscrupulous ETs or it didn't really happen the way I remember it or that it didn't even happen at all.

Indeed, during those periods when I am alone with my thoughts, when the house is quiet and my mood pensive, when I am nagged by self-doubt, I begin to wonder if even the memories of what I had for lunch the day before can be trusted. Is it possible that memories that we are so sure of, that are so real, that actually help to define who we are, could be counterfeit? Can they be invented or even implanted by an outside source, by aliens with sinister motives or nefarious humans—government agents or otherwise—with secret technologies that are unknown to the general population?

To shake me from these spirals of despair, from losing faith in my own perceived reality and beliefs, I need only return to my mailbag of letters and e-mail or to recall the many conversations I've had with others to remind myself that I am not alone.

I am not alone. There is so much comfort in that thought. Many readers have thanked me for telling my story, for in doing so I have given confirmation to their own personal experiences, have helped excise self-doubts about their own states of mind, and have reassured them that there are others like them—many others. Indeed, there hardly remains any middle ground: Either these hundreds and even thousands of contacts and sightings are really happening, or the world is witnessing an outbreak of delusions on a pandemic scale, making it one of the biggest, virtually unreported sociological and medical stories of the millennium. Frankly, I find that scenario even more fantastic to contemplate than the fact that we may not be the only inhabited planet in the universe. And while I am still trying to come to terms with my own experience, I do believe that the ET/abduction phenomenon is real, and further, I find it deplorable that so few outside the community of those directly affected are taking it seriously.

Perhaps the best way I can put it comes from a scene in Carl Sagan's novel *Contact*. The character played by Jodie Foster in the movie version says after her space travel adventure:

"I had an experience. I can't prove it. I can't even explain it. But everything that I know as a human being, everything that I am, tells me that it was real."

I too had an experience. I can't prove it. I can't explain it. All I can do is report it, and allow you too to grapple—as I have—with the challenge of contact.

—Phillip H. Krapf
Southern California
April 2001

Recap of My Initial Contact

This book is the sequel to *The Contact Has Begun*, the story of my initial three-day encounter aboard a starship with a very advanced race of extraterrestrial beings who come from a planet whose name would translate into English as "Verdant." For those who are new to this story, I will use this introduction to provide a synopsis of my original contact with this species that I call, naturally, Verdants. Beginning then in chapter 1, I will launch into the continuing story of the unusual series of contacts that led up to my second visit to their ship, which they call the *Goodwill*, in early 2000. *The Challenge of Contact* describes my new experiences as reporter for the Verdants' contact project. It also gives an update on the Verdants' timetable for formal and public contact with the people of our planet, which will initially occur through disclosure of contact with the Verdants by hundreds of world leaders they have recruited to act as interplanetary ambassadors. Again, I am simply the reporter for this unfolding drama—indeed, one whose role was to come into question, as you will see later in this book.

It all began in June 1997 when I awoke in the middle of the night and found myself encased in a luminous shaft of light, then involuntarily beamed aboard an alien spacecraft. Within a matter of seconds I was standing before the strangest creatures I had ever seen, though not so different from depictions of alien beings that others have given. They were just over five feet tall, with dark, narrow eyes, nearly imperceptible noses, no visible body hair, and skin tones from grayish white to slightly tan. They were wearing satiny robes of varying muted colors. They even spoke to me in English, though their thin lips didn't move. What a stunning scene it was—or at least, one would have thought so. As a lifelong skeptic and nonbeliever in UFOs and alien-abduction tales, this experience should have struck me with shocking force, but it wasn't shock that I felt. Oddly, I simply felt at peace, and fully alert.

Deep down, I suppose I knew in that instant what had happened to me—no amount of denial could alter the fact that I had apparently been abducted, I was on a spacecraft, and I was among extraterrestrials—but my psyche just wasn't responding as one might expect. As I wrote in the first book, "whenever I had given even passing attention to these stories, I thought that such an experience would not be survivable, that the human mind would simply snap at the shock and immediately plunge into an abyss of insanity."

Previous to this extraordinary experience, I had virtually no knowledge of UFO phenomenon. The limited information that I did have came from the mainstream press. I did know that physical examinations of some sort were one thread that tied many abduction stories together (and in fact the room I was first in had scores of tables with humans on most of them, attended by white-garbed aliens), and so I quickly concluded that I had been taken aboard for that same purpose.

Nevertheless, the fact that I was completely at peace, barren of any fear, seemed to belie the reality. The strongest emotion I felt at the time was rather one of intense curiosity. It then occurred to me that my sensibilities, my consciousness, must have been altered. Otherwise, how could I reconcile my actual demeanor with the uncontrolled reaction that, by all human standards, would be normal under such circumstances? Why was I accepting this unimaginable scenario with such equanimity? As I would learn later, the beam of light through which I had I traveled to the ship had somehow triggered a calming effect that prepared my psyche to accept the initial contact.

Unlike those on the tables before me, however, I quickly found out that I was on board this strange ship for another reason. The Verdants, who claim to have come from a planet some 14 million light-years from Earth (the name of their planet apparently translates into "Verdant" in English, which I interpreted to mean something akin to "garden planet"), said that they had been recruiting hundreds of humans to serve as liaisons for an impending summit conference between representatives of our two species. People from all walks of life, from every area of human endeavor—many of them leaders in their fields—were being enlisted to help lay the groundwork for the contact between the two species.

Those being recruited for liaison purposes as interplanetary diplomats, as it were, will perform essential tasks to help prepare Earth for contact; they were given the title of Ambassador. A similar number of more anonymous individuals have been invited to play supporting or secondary roles, and were given the title of Deputy Envoy. I am a part of this second group, apparently chosen on the basis of a personal recommendation from a staff person at the *Los Angeles Times* who had been recruited as an Ambassador (referred to in my first book as "X"). The *Times* is where the bulk of my newspaper career took place before I retired in 1993.

I spent most of my waking hours on the ship being briefed by the Verdants in orientation sessions. During my stay, I had a personal tour guide and attendant who went by the name of Gina. The other key figure among the Verdants with whom I had contact was using the name Gus. These names were adopted for my benefit because I was incapable of addressing them by their real names in their native tongue.

I learned in the orientation sessions that the Verdants have been space explorers for millions of years. In the beginning, they didn't know if they were alone in the universe until they began coming across other civilizations. Eventually, they joined with a handful of these other advanced species to form the Intergalactic Federation of Sovereign Planets (IFSP). Over the eons, as new civilizations were discovered and brought into the fold, the organization continued to grow until it reached its current membership of approximately 27,000 different species on as many different planets. The Verdants, however, told me that they have "colonized" a great number of formerly uninhabited planets. ("Colonize" is actually my word for what I think was closer to something like "terraformed"—making uninhabited and uninhabitable planets more habitable or more hospitable.)

The Verdants and a number of other species have developed the technology and the ability to engage in a constant search for life in the universe, exploring, mapping, and cataloguing as they go. Planets that contain higher forms of life are classified according to the inhabitants' level of development; those species with high intelligence, especially if they have developed complex civilizations, receive the most scrutiny. Once a planet with higher life forms is discovered, the Verdants take up positions in that particular solar system and begin a period of observation and study that can last anywhere from several weeks to hundreds of years. The ones requiring the shortest period of study are those that are still considered to be at least 10,000 years away from developing the capabilities of space flight. The planet is catalogued and the exploration party moves on; several thousand years may pass before it's revisited. Those civilizations that have progressed to the point where they are within 1,000 years of developing the technology for space flight are assigned a permanent observation party. The purpose is to ensure that the species under study does not pose a threat to any other cosmic civilization once it embarks into space. (Species that are aggressive and hostile are kept isolated on their home planets until such time as they may evolve into a peaceful race and pose no threat to their neighbors. One cardinal, universal rule is that no weapons are allowed into space.) The observation team will then study and chronicle the history, the cultures, the technology, the languages, the environment, and the psychological, physiological and anatomical makeup of the inhabitants.

When a civilization is on the verge of taking its first preliminary steps into space, the Verdants determine whether it's suitable for admission to the IFSP. By this time, of course, the explorers will have learned everything there is to know about the planet and its people. If admission is granted, preparations are made for contact. Each ship monitoring a planet has an ad hoc committee to coordinate this effort. The observation party will then guide the species through the final critical stages to ensure a smooth transition into its new interstellar reality.

To the best of my knowledge, Earth is under the Verdants' jurisdiction—strictly as an object of observation—since it was a Verdant ship and crew that first discovered it. The Verdants, however, are not the only ones monitoring emerging civilizations. Other species are engaged in the same pursuit, a routine part of the IFSP organizational structure and mission. I do not know if any of these other species are in Earth's neighborhood because this was never discussed with me.

In the last decade of the 20th century, the Verdants concluded that humankind, having advanced to the point where it was rapidly developing the technology for entering deep space, was qualified for membership in the federation. There was, however, one primary sticking point. For the crossover to be successful, it was necessary for the 80 percent of the human population who have tried to lead decent, thoughtful, creative lives to gain control over the 20 percent who are largely responsible for the planet's ills because of their greed, lack of ethics, or whatever else makes them a threat to a just and loving world. They didn't provide tactics or strategies on just how to achieve this, asserting instead that our destiny is in our own hands and they have no intention of interfering. Observation thus continued through the end of the '90s to monitor the progress of this expected transformation and plans were laid for contact to take place in the first decade of the 21st century.

The Summit Timetable

In preparation, each Ambassador has been assigned a specific duty and will be required to draw up and submit to the Verdants a detailed blueprint that they would use to carry out their varied assignments. These proposals will form a basic component of the groundwork upon which the whole operation rests, involving monumental logistical and planning challenges because of the importance and critical nature of each step leading up to contact. Many of the Ambassadors must continue to hold down their full-time jobs while taking on this arduous and time-consuming task. As a consequence, the Verdants are allowing as much time as the Ambassadors need to compile their reports.

(I should mention that initially Ambassadors were expected to complete their reports within three years, according to the Ambassador who spelled out the timetable in more detail upon my return from the ship. And then, after a six-month period during which the Verdants would assimilate the input of their human counterparts, the public phase of the contact project would begin. However, the events reported in this book point to new controversies that have arisen regarding the timetable and the feasibility of the contact. The upshot, given my encounters with Verdants and Ambassadors upon my second visit to the ship, is that the Verdants appear determined to go forward with the contact—or at the least a decision for contact—"some time in the near future." Personally, I remain optimistic that the contact will take place as scheduled.)

The optimistic scenario is as follows: After they have received all the Ambassador reports, the Verdants will process and modify the plans as necessary. The plans will then be returned to each individual Ambassador for actual implementation. Over the following year or so, all Ambassadors worldwide will begin revealing their roles in the planning of the impending summit meeting and contact with the extraterrestrials. They will also begin meeting with and briefing their various Earth contacts: government officials, leaders in science, technology, law, communications, education, the arts, medicine, politics, commerce, manufacturing, and a host of others.

They will be speaking out, granting interviews, explaining their experiences and employing their credibility and influence to persuade the masses of Earth inhabitants of the legitimacy of the story.

In the years following, if all goes according to schedule, a new city, tentatively referred to as Genesis, will be constructed somewhere in the American Southwest. The compound will contain living quarters, recreation areas, meeting rooms, educational laboratories, public schools for the children of human inhabitants, libraries, a university, a landing site for alien shuttle craft, a traditional international airport, commercial establishments, maintenance facilities, and a government center. No need will go unmet. It will be a completely self-contained community.

It is here that the first formal contact between the two species will take place as the emissaries of all the nations on Earth and the delegates of the star travelers convene. After formal introductions and opening ceremonies, the representatives of both worlds will interact in both business and social settings, after which the heads of government will return to their duties in their respective capitals while their hand-picked emissaries will stay behind to continue negotiations and planning. The total process will take at least a year to complete.

As the temporary residents depart, permanent residents will take their place and Genesis will continue to function as a modern international center and the planet's first interstellar city. Each government will select a number of volunteer representatives from every imaginable field of human endeavor to participate in an intensive orientation program. They will live in Genesis for the duration of the program, which will last for one to three years depending upon their specialties and field of study. Each morning, from Monday to Friday, they will board a shuttlecraft and spend the day in classrooms aboard the *Goodwill,* the ship I was on. These are the people who will lead the human race through the transition from isolated earthling to member of the intergalactic community of star travelers.

Once humankind's training is complete, the human species will be formerly inducted into the Intergalactic Federation of Sovereign Planets. All new members of the IFSP are subject to a probationary period of 10 Verdant years—about 27 Earth years—under tight supervision. During this time the initiates must operate under a specific set of restrictions. One of those is a limitation on access to other star travelers' technologies. For example, the Verdants' propulsion system—which I call the 'Flicker Drive' for lack of a technological name—allows them to maneuver around the barrier of space at a rate of *one million times* the speed of light, as they told me on my first visit. The reason for such a restriction is probably due to security concerns. If we fail to pass probation and must remain confined to our home planet, we would in effect be classified as unsuitable for the time being for space travel. Access to certain "secret technologies" would clearly violate such a condition.

All of this information was shared over three days of intense meetings during which the Verdants told me who they are, where they come from, why they are here, and what the people of Earth can expect to experience during the next decade or so leading up to the official meeting between the two species. I was asked to write a "white paper" outlining in general terms the details of these developments. I agreed, and the white paper was released as a book in early 1998—*The Contact Has Begun*. (A revised edition featuring an extensive new Epilogue came out in mid-1999.)

I never expected to write a sequel, of course, but as improbable as it seems, I was taken up to the ship again. I am compelled to tell this story because I feel it's important; there is new information to share, and much is at stake. I was not prompted by the Verdants to do this, and in fact I wrote it with mixed feelings.

Even as I was writing the first book, I knew I would pay a price for going public. It was easy to visualize what *my* reaction would have been if someone I knew had written such a book during that part of my life when I openly scoffed at such tales. But where I expected to be subjected to some good-natured ribbing, I got a bit of a bloody nose instead. It really stung, but that's to be expected. I smiled wryly through it all.

There were severed and strained friendships and relationships. The local newspaper had a jolly good time lampooning me. Both UFO and mainstream media, including some book reviewers, threw a few jabs at my chin and tender nose.

The wildest and most outrageous material—the bulk of it sheer nonsense—emanated from the internet, which is not surprising considering the chaotic nature of that medium. It is a fount of misinformation and disinformation. I was taken aback when I discovered that the UFO-alien/abduction community is rife with strident dissension and personal feuding—where lies, rumors both founded and unfounded, character assaults, charges and countercharges, calumny, and slander are routinely thrown around. But compared to how some others in the community are subjected to a constant pummeling, I have been treated gently.

Before the advent of the Internet, a person who believed that he had been unfairly portrayed could contact the offending publication and demand satisfaction in the form of a retraction or correction. Lacking that, he or she could turn to the courts for redress. But while most major publications are staffed by professionals who abide by certain standards of decorum and responsibility, the internet is so uncontrolled, so accessible to every malcontent with an ax to grind that there is no way for a damaged person to fight back. Add the element of anonymity and the worldwide nature of the beast—in which false information picked up and spread by hundreds of others of like mind can circle the globe in a matter of seconds— and it is evident that any effort to try to find and hold someone accountable is an extremely difficult exercise.

Whenever the subject comes up, I tell people to be very judicious and discriminating in assessing any information they find on the Internet. To be sure, there are legitimate professional news organizations that have web sites, and the material on those sites can be regarded as just as reliable as the information that appears in the sponsor's publication. But anything that doesn't emanate from a reputable and reliable news source—such as a major metropolitan newspaper, prestigious news magazines, respectable and respected TV and radio news departments—I view with skepticism. The information could be true, but it also could be as totally unreliable as the gossip that is created, transmuted, and wantonly spread by the most scandalous and uninformed elements of society.

Imagine a newspaper or magazine staffed by professional journalists in which any malcontent or moron were allowed to waltz in off the street and post any story he wanted in the publication. The reader wouldn't know what to believe. That is the sorry state of the Internet today.

To be on the safe side, I don't believe a word I read on it unless it comes from a reliable, reputable source and/or until I can independently verify the information or find reputable corroboration for it.

I don't think it's any secret that certain special interests opposed to public scrutiny of the UFO phenomenon have planted moles inside the community to spy, construct dossiers, disrupt, and engage in other practices that would discredit the entire phenomenon. The Internet is a great way to do this.

Although I knew I carried a burden of responsibility for standing up to the criticism, I would be less than forthright if I didn't admit that there were periods when the negative reaction raised grave doubts in my mind about the nature of my experience. It was at those times that I entertained the possibility that perhaps it was all a delusion. But almost miraculously, whenever I was feeling at my lowest, someone who had lived through a similar experience would contact me and my spirits would soar. Just knowing that I was not alone—and being reminded of it—had an invigorating effect and helped to erase my doubts.

Dozens of people have used the word "courage" to describe my decision to come forward, but I still take exception to that characterization. After all, I'm retired and don't have to subject myself to daily ridicule from colleagues. Nor do I have to worry about being denied pay increases or promotions. The truth is, if I were still employed at the time of my first experience, I don't know that I would have had the courage to do what I did.

But I stand by my story, and am comforted by the hope that I have played even a small part in enabling the historic summit of the Verdant race and the human race to come to fruition—through this, my second report on these unprecedented events of interplanetary diplomacy.

The Challenge of Contact

part 1

a walk in the park

On April 2, 1999, a Good Friday—some 22 months after my first encounter with the Verdant race—I awoke about 6:30 a.m. in a very odd state of mind. I could feel myself lying in bed in my physical body, yet I knew that I was inhabiting another plane of existence beyond my normal senses. Strangely enough, this was a place where I felt completely at home, as if I truly belonged there. My mind was crystal clear, and in that clarity I understood with a purity of thought unlike anything I'd experienced before that I was in an exotic space, pulled over from my ordinary state of consciousness by some unknown force.

I didn't sense any spoken words. I don't believe that I even cognitively thought of the idea on my own. A specific thought was just suddenly there in my mind:

"*Seek out the angel and you will be sought in return.*"

I knew instinctively, perhaps even intellectually—certainly emotionally—that I had received a message, and its meaning mystified me. But a series of events soon occurred that convinced me I had a mission to perform, a mission that would lead me on a strange and enigmatic journey. It would take me the very next day to the San Francisco Bay Area—for an encounter with an angel and an Ambassador—and eventually back into outer space aboard an extraterrestrial starship.

Almost instinctively—at least it felt instinctive—I knew what I had to do. I telephoned my wife at work and told her that we would be driving up to San Francisco for the Easter weekend.

"Well, that's pretty sudden," she said. "What brought this on?"

"Just an impulse," I responded. In fact I was possessed by an urgent beckoning telling me I was supposed to be there. It came from that same unknown force that had invaded my consciousness with thoughts that needed no words to direct me.

On Saturday morning we were on the road by 7 a.m. During the drive, she barraged me with questions over this sudden impulse. I was noncommittal, saying only that I thought it would be nice for us to get away for a few days. Secretly I was *seeking out the angel,* though I didn't know where I was going or what I would do once I got there—if I ever did. I just obeyed my instincts, sensing that some vague but powerful force was guiding me.

Five hours later we swung across the Oakland Bay Bridge into San Francisco, met a friend downtown, and spent an enjoyable afternoon talking, lunching, driving and walking.

Suddenly, as we were driving around the city, a word popped into my mind, seemingly unattached to any existing train of thought—"pinhole."

I didn't have a clue as to its meaning.

Catching the eye of our friend in the rearview mirror, I asked, "What does 'pinhole' refer to?"

"Manhole?"

"No, pinhole," I repeated. "Is there an area of the city known as pinhole?"

"Pinhole. Pinhole. No, that's a new one on me."

"Isn't there a Presidio?" my wife asked.

"No, that's not what I was thinking of. I don't think so, anyway."

Our friend then rattled off a slew of districts in the city: Noe Valley, the Castro, the Haight, the Marina, Pacific Heights, Nob Hill, Russian Hill, North Beach, Cole Valley, the Tenderloin. None of them struck a chord, so I decided to drop the subject. I wasn't getting anywhere and it was just frustrating me.

After a moment, though, she casually mentioned that there is a town on the East Bay called Pinole.

Eureka! *That* felt right, that was the place I wanted to go. But the day was late, so I forced myself to wait until morning.

The next day, after dropping my wife off at her friend's house, I headed north, and by 11 a.m. I was in the town of

Pinole. I found a municipal parking lot, got out of my car, and started walking.

It was Easter morning, not an especially important day to an atheist, but at this stage, having come in contact with aliens—and ones who spoke of God, of all things—I wasn't sure what I believed anymore. In fact, I can say honestly that deep in my soul—whose existence I was now willing to consider—I realized that I had changed. I knew that I would never look upon the universe, and my own place in it, in the same way again. I had been so sure of my place in the world and now I was filled with doubts, with questions for which I had no easy answers.

Almost overnight I had gone from being an outspoken skeptic on matters of UFOs and alien abductions to becoming not only a believer in such phenomena but an actual participant in an extraterrestrial adventure. And that's on top of having my belief system—or, nonbelief, to be more precise—shaken to the core with respect to things metaphysical. I longed to find some structure, some purpose, some meaning that would explain the extraordinary events of the last two years.

Pinole felt virtually deserted, perhaps because of the religious holiday. Most of the shops I saw appeared closed. I'm sure the churches were full. At first, Pinole struck me as a blue-collar town, but as I looked deeper while driving around I realized that while many of the houses appeared old, they were not neglected. I thought that because of its superb location and enviable weather, many commuters with upscale jobs in the bigger Bay Area cities would find it an attractive place of refuge.

I roamed aimlessly for awhile, then returned to my car

and drove around. Still seeking out the angel, I passed a number of parks and finally pulled the car to a curb and walked into one, taking a seat on a bench in the shade of a tree. I don't know why I picked this particular park; it just felt right to me. There were a handful of people, some of them with small children. I sat back and enjoyed the cool serenity and sylvan peacefulness. The pace was just right—slow and relaxing. Five minutes passed.

At first, I took little notice of the man who approached and sat down next to me. When he spoke, I was startled and reflexively flinched.

"Beautiful day," he said.

Terrific," I responded.

He was dressed casually in jeans, with a plaid shirt under his windbreaker and white athletic shoes. Although he looked vaguely familiar, I was pretty sure we had never met. He looked to be in his forties, with a chiseled face and a full head of brown hair that stirred in the breeze. His eyes were an undistinguished, everyday blue.

"How was your drive?" he asked.

"Not bad," I answered before giving any thought to the question.

Then suddenly I turned to look at him. I was certain at that moment that my quest had been fulfilled. I stared mutely and waited for him to speak further.

"Another person will join us shortly." He lowered his voice as a young couple strolled by hand-in-hand. "I should fill you in on him. He's an Ambassador and he has information for you."

"And you are . . . ?" I asked, my voice trailing off.

"I go by the name of Paul." He reached out his hand,

which I shook firmly.

I didn't see any point in mincing words. I wanted solid, understandable, uncomplicated answers. I had been operating for two days on feelings, hunches, and irresolute beckonings. Suddenly feeling feisty, the words spilled out of me in a torrent. I wanted to know who he was and what his purpose was for meeting me. I asked if I had received some sort of telepathic communication that had steered me to this place hundreds of miles from my home and, if so, for what reason. I went on and on, and it wasn't until I had finished, as I reflected upon my outburst, that I realized I had been acting like a whiny schoolchild.

Naturally, I wasn't taking notes, so I can't quote extensively. But I do remember proclaiming at various points that "I hate being jacked around," and "I'm getting tired of the games." At one point I also complained in frustration that "sometimes I wish that I had never gotten mixed up in this business," or words very similar to that.

Mixed into the equation, I have to admit, is an inherent and abiding dislike of getting the runaround by people from whom I am trying to extract information. That goes back to my reporting days when I was trying to sniff out a story and had to constantly battle to cut through the evasions, the temporizing, the half-truths, and the misinformation that the spin doctors tried to feed me. Actually, I got pretty good at cutting through the rubbish—in the interest of civility, I won't use the scatological vulgarity that is commonly used in such cases—that some interviewees throw at reporters. I learned to recognize the snow job, blow it off, and ask the kind of penetrating questions that yielded the hard information that I was after.

Paul bided his time while I vented my frustration. When he spoke, his tone was understanding, and at one point he put a sympathetic hand on my shoulder while he talked. At the same time, he made it very clear that, yes, he was there for a purpose, I was there for a purpose, he would decide what information I was to receive, and no amount of adolescent petulance on my part was going to change that.

Despite all of my probing questions, he supplied me with only the scantiest personal information, referring to himself as only "an intermediary." I never did figure out in this meeting if he was an Ambassador himself or what other role he might be playing in this cosmic drama. During our time together, though, it was clear that he was well versed in the area of spirituality. If I had to guess about his vocation, I would have said that he was a man of the cloth or perhaps a religious scholar.

I had an urge to ask him for proof of his connection with the Verdants. I didn't know who he was or whether I was being manipulated or tricked into talking to someone I shouldn't be and revealing confidential information. Then I realized how absurd this idea was. It would be impossible for an impostor to know where to find me, to know so much about me, and to be aware of the forces that had led me to this place. After all, he had approached me right out of the blue.

No, he was authentic, all right. He was also a mystery. Yet despite his refusal to answer many of my questions, I couldn't help feeling—not thinking, but feeling—that he was a most remarkable and fascinating individual. He radiated a quality that I couldn't quite put my finger on: a certain exceptional presence.

Paul talked and I listened. I learned that every effort was being made to keep all Ambassadors and Deputy Envoys posted on developments that had a direct bearing on their roles. In my case, this briefing was apparently a matter of courtesy to keep me apprised in general on the progress of the plan, or so I thought at the time.

Paul did confirm that I had been contacted telepathically and led to this park. When I asked him why the message and the process had been so cloaked in ambiguity, he said something to the effect that telepathic messages sometimes do not translate as literally as they are transmitted, especially when being received by those with little or no experience with that medium. The messages are often received by the intended recipient in the form of metaphors and symbols, such as those that are found in dreams. The ability to translate them varies with the individual.

He touched on a dozen topics during a discourse that went on for several hours, waxing at times philosophical about the condition of the world and humankind's future. The turn of the century was just around the corner and he made several predictions that in hindsight turned out to be true. There would be no Second Coming, no Rapture, no Armageddon, and no Y2K calamity, he declared. At one point, after musing about rumors of planned mass suicides when the clock ticked 2000, he clasped his hands behind his head, stretched out his long legs, and as though he were discussing nothing more important than the weather, said, "The ways of humans are so very strange."

It wasn't the meaning behind the words that struck me but rather his detached manner in saying them. It was as though he were speaking as a mere observer of the human race, not as a part of it. It was an intensely eerie feeling. Eventually, a man whom I had noticed walking in the park earlier stopped in front of us. He was wearing a suit and tie, certainly appropriate attire for an Easter Sunday. Paul and I stood up.

"This is John," he said to me, and the man extended a hand.

"Let me guess. John Doe," I said.

"Or Smith, or Jones, but you can call me Chip if you prefer," the man said as we exchanged a handshake.

"And you're an Ambassador," I said.

I studied his face carefully, and although he did look slightly familiar, I couldn't place it with any of the pictures that I had seen in the ambassadorial roster. That didn't surprise me; there were only a handful of faces that I could conjure up from the roster, and that was only because I had been familiar with them prior to my journey to the starship.

"I'll leave you two to talk," Paul said as Chip took his place on the bench. "We'll meet another time at another place." He began to walk away.

"Wait a minute," I called after him. He turned and waved, but kept walking. I had a million more questions for him. I looked helplessly at Chip, who beckoned me to sit down.

I took off my glasses and rubbed a palm across my closed eyes, massaging my temples as well. I don't see much without my specs. The world turns into a fuzzy, unfocused kaleidoscope of shapes, forms, and smears of colors. I don't even have depth perception and have never experienced that phenomenon; my left eye is crossed and both eyes don't work together to form a stereoscopic image. I have had this condition for a lifetime.

But suddenly, as I watched Paul walk away, the scene in front of me sharpened into crystal clear focus. I was experiencing depth perception for the first time in all of its breathtaking glory! The image was nothing short of miraculous. Looking out upon this simple earthly landscape—seeing the image as three-dimensional in which objects projected themselves into space so that I could judge size, thickness, form, and distance—was mesmerizing. My world normally passes before me as a flat field, much as one would see life on a movie screen. But to see the images jump out of that screen was more breathtaking than I could ever have imagined. The experience stirred in me emotions that were every bit as strong and moving as those I felt when I first gazed upon the full grandeur of the universe from the observation bubble of the Verdant ship. My knees had literally buckled when I was confronted by the billions of stars and galaxies that studded the infinite blackness of space like gemstones. They would have given way now as well if I weren't sitting down.

And then, just as suddenly, my vision returned to normal—blurry, flat, unfocused. I put my glasses back on. Mysteriously, Paul had disappeared from sight. Yet I should have been able to see him: He still had some way to go before the path took him out of view. I was totally bewildered. The event had occurred so suddenly and unexpectedly and was over so quickly—no more than three to five seconds—that I thought I might have been hallucinating.

I became annoyed with myself: always the rational mind, always seeking a logical explanation for the unexplainable. But this was no hallucination.

This was nothing short of a miracle.

It was Easter Sunday, and I had literally seen the light. I can't say that I "got religion." It was more like a spiritual awakening to some of the wonders that had been missing from my life. I wasn't resurrected, but I was convinced that I had been touched, by . . . something.

I wanted to talk about the incident to Chip, but I found myself incapable of doing so. If any experience called for sharing, this one certainly had to qualify. And yet, though reeling psychologically and emotionally from the impact, I was overwhelmed with the conviction that to analyze what happened would somehow violate the sacredness of it. So I kept it to myself.

Chip and I spent hours together, occasionally getting up to stroll leisurely through the park. He did most of the talking, although he was more inclined to address my questions than Paul had been, and slightly more willing to reveal personal information about himself. He also delved into areas that had a significant, and even worrisome, bearing on me in my capacity as a minor spokesman, of sorts, for the Verdants. That is, even though I am merely a secondary player in the program, I had stuck my neck out while the major players still remained shrouded in the security blanket of anonymity.

While there was nothing specifically said that I could point to as reasons for my moments of unease, there was a tone that had me on edge at times. Perhaps I was overreacting.

Chip told me he was an official at a Silicon Valley computer firm (I am trying to say as little about him as possible) and was deeply engrossed in projects that essentially commanded his full attention. He didn't come right out and say so, but I got the impression that he was recruited for his professional expertise and his respectable standing in the field of science and technology. That's why I believed him when he informed me that, thanks to briefings of key Ambassadors by the Verdants, human scientists and technicians had been provided the necessary information to forestall most major disruptions as a result of the so-called Y2K problem. And indeed, the remarkably anticlimactic turn of the century, especially following the urgent warnings of potential chaos that preceded it, suggests such plausibility.

Over the next several hours, our dialogue touched on a host of subjects, including reincarnation, telepathy, crop circles, and cattle mutilations. Paul claimed that the cattle mutilations are the handiwork of humans and that the authorities would soon reveal incontrovertible evidence to that effect; there may even be some arrests, he said.

During the afternoon I also learned that some opponents of the contact, both foreign and domestic, have compiled enemies lists containing the names of many prominent UFO activists, and that I have the dubious honor of being included on some of those rosters. Ironically, some of those who oppose the contact actually belong to UFO groups, he told me. He called them infiltrators, whose purpose is to cause disruption within the community. This revelation led me to remember several incidents of people at conferences who pressed too hard, who seemed motivated by more than curiosity to extract information from me. Could some of them have been so-called plants?

Somewhere along the line, Chip mentioned X and asked if he and I were still in contact. I replied that I hadn't seen or heard from him since April 1998.

In *The Contact Has Begun*, I mentioned that a person from the *Los Angeles Times* who had been chosen as an Ambassador had been instrumental in persuading the Verdants to recruit me to write the white paper publicly announcing their presence in Earth's neighborhood. In addition, I also mentioned that I had met aboard the ship another human, a very important figure, whom I recognized immediately as we both were taking a tour of the craft during an informal period. I also wrote that I had been shown a roster of many of the important people who had been recruited as Ambassadors, which was a virtual Who's Who of the World.

After I returned from the ship, the Ambassador from the *Times,* whom I referred to as X, contacted me to arrange a luncheon meeting and compare notes. This occurred in September 1997. I also had several other conversations with X subsequent to that. Let me pause here and relate the most important of these.

In mid-April of 1998, I answered the doorbell one morning and found myself facing X along with another man. This was unusual because our previous meetings had all been arranged beforehand. There was a sense of urgency about his manner as I invited him in. He introduced me to "John," and we exchanged handshakes. I put on the kettle for tea, and soon we were seated at the kitchen table.

"John what?" I asked casually, taking note of the nervousness that was evident in a slight trembling of his hand that rattled the teacup against the saucer as he drank.

Before he could answer, X replied. "John Doe."

"Ah, a mystery," I said with a good-natured smile. X eyed me with a slight smile of his own. John, whom I am not at liberty to describe other than to say he is not American, was quiet while X and I chatted amiably about nothing consequential. Then he got around to the reason for their visit, and his demeanor took a more serious turn.

"It is imperative," X said in a firm voice, "that you recognize how important it is for you to exercise extreme caution when discussing me, the Ambassador you met on the ship, the ambassadorial roster, and the timetable."

The words came across almost as a warning, and caught me totally off guard. He said I could talk only on those subjects about which I had already written, but that I was not to elaborate or expand upon them.

I asked him timidly if I had done something wrong, spoken out of turn, broken any confidences, or revealed any secrets. He softened his tone and assured me that I had committed no violations of protocol and that the purpose of his visit was preemptive. Nevertheless, while X appeared reasonably calm, John was less so, certainly nervous, possibly even agitated.

X told me that John was—or, at least had been—an Ambassador. I had already guessed that; indeed, I couldn't imagine his being here talking so frankly and openly with someone who was not intimately involved in the adventure. The primary message, repeated by X and boiled down to its essentials, was simply to reinforce the need to be discreet and avoid revealing certain material that was still considered confidential, which I thought I had been doing all along.

X sipped his tea and eyed me over the rim of the cup.

"We just wanted to make sure you understood," he said. "Have you had any strange visitors, noticed anybody watching you or following you? Anything suspicious going on like late-night phone calls, anonymous mail, strangers approaching you to strike up conversations, people pumping you for information?"

"Nothing out of the ordinary that I'm aware of," I said tentatively. "You mean like 'Men in Black'?"

My attempt at frivolity was met with grim looks; they weren't in a whimsical mood. Actually, there had been a few minor incidents and communications that caused me some concern at the time, such as vague warnings that no one could be trusted. But no problems ever developed as a result, so I didn't bother mentioning them.

"Why? Should I be expecting something? What's going on?" I wasn't really alarmed, but a slight edge had crept into my voice.

"Oh, there's a lot going on, much more than you realize," X replied. "If I had a couple of days, I still couldn't fill you in completely. And even I don't know everything that's happening."

It turned out that the two men were part of a network of small teams who were calling on a select number of recruits to assess, advise, and update, on a need-to-know basis, developments surrounding the program and the rate at which the plan was going forward. I learned that some emissaries had been harassed and had run into other unspecified problems. I was strongly advised to be cautious when picking up mail from my post office box, to make sure I wasn't being watched. The bottom-line message I was getting was to be vigilant, and I vowed to be more careful, although at that moment I couldn't imagine why anyone would want to tail me.

I really got the point, though, when X told me that John, in his own country, was nearly forced into a car that had pulled up beside him on the street. Fortunately, he was able to make a run for it and escape. Certainly the incident could be viewed as an attempted kidnapping, but John couldn't imagine what the purpose was or what the end result would have been. Perhaps he was merely going to be questioned, but he also had to consider the possibility that he might never have been heard from again.

This revelation disturbed me. When I pressed them for details, my questions were brushed off. What they did volunteer was that word about John's association with the Verdants had gotten out. John admitted that it probably was his own fault; his tongue had become loose one evening with a close friend over drinks. Two weeks later the kidnapping attempt was made.

John believed that he had been "outed." The attempt to force him into the car, he said, was not merely a random street crime. He felt he had lost his effectiveness to continue serving as an Ambassador and decided to go into hiding.

"There aren't many nations where at least one copy of your book isn't available," John said. "Any government leader who wished to see it could easily get hold of it. There are some very powerful forces who do not want this contact to take place, and they will resort to extreme measures to stop it."

Major opposition to contact comes from, among others, leaders of rogue nations who see it as a threat to their power base. But there also are domestic groups and individuals, X said, who don't welcome the idea of extraterrestrial contact. Some are conspiracy theorists who see secret agents under every bed. There are others who believe that the aliens are intent on setting up a one-world government whose human leaders would do the bidding of their alien puppet masters. Other resistance comes from more "mainstream" people who have certain religious, economic, or political agendas and beliefs that would be threatened by an extraterrestrial presence and all it implied.

Still others aren't convinced that the aliens have the best interests of humans at heart, or they simply have reservations—very real personal concerns—that motivate them to proceed with extreme caution. And there are those who are firmly convinced that the aliens are in fact diabolical. These people could be described as planetary isolationists who fear contact of any kind and who want no part of it. In fact, I was told, this group actually poses more of a threat than the former because it is highly effective at working within the system to achieve its ends.

I asked if I was in any danger, but both men assured me that they had no knowledge of any plot against me. They emphasized that the primary purpose of their visit was simply to let me know that loose talk on my part, while not necessarily putting me in danger, could compromise the missions of others, particularly foreigners, and possibly even put those people in jeopardy. I assured my guests again that I would be a model of discretion in my talks and interviews, and would be constantly on the alert for suspicious activity.

But what in the world do I know about questionable activity, I wondered. Should I be suspicious if a new postal carrier begins delivering my mail? And what should I do if I do notice such a change? Call the FBI or the CIA? File a police report? Go into hiding whenever the mail truck comes up the street? Despite the gravity of the situation, there was a part of me that saw the whole thing as a third-rate Hollywood melodrama.

Both men rose, and it was clear that our meeting had ended—amicably, I had thought. But as I walked them to the door, I casually asked X why I had to be so careful in talking about the timetable.

His demeanor suddenly shifted, and a kind of cold-bloodedness entered his eyes. He responded with a forced calm that it was no accident that I had come away from the ship with only a hazy notion of the timetable leading up to contact.

"You got the timetable from me," he said. "There's nothing that can be done about that. Just do me a favor and try to avoid talking about it."

I was confused. There was no rational reason for his sudden turn in mood.

"How can I do that?" I asked. "It's in the book, it's no secret."

"Humor me." He stared silently at me for several seconds, appearing to fight for control.

"This isn't about you," he went on in a measured tone. "There are some very important people who have more on the line than you do. Some of them are already confiding in colleagues and government officials. A few others will be going public in the months and years to come. They will be staking their reputations on this enterprise and they have a lot to lose if things don't go forward as expected."

I asked him if I could at least explain to audiences why

I had to tiptoe around these certain subjects.

"No!" he snapped. "How can you? You don't know the reason because I haven't told you."

"No, you misunderstand," I said lamely. "I know I don't know why, but, I mean, is it okay to tell people that I've been told not to talk?"

"Someday. Not now. I need at least a year. Just generalize. I'm sure you'll figure something out."

I was completely mystified by his reaction. Obviously I had touched a nerve. I felt as though I should apologize, but I didn't know for what. Even so, I made a half-hearted attempt, but he quickly brushed off my effort. I didn't want to make an enemy of him, and I didn't want him to leave on this sour note. But he strode toward his car with John on his heels, and then they were gone.

I had been silent for several moments as I thought about the dramatic last conversation I had had with X, but I was brought back to the present as Chip's voice broke through to my consciousness.

"We're having a little bit of a problem with X," Chip explained. "To be brutally frank, there are complications as well with several other key Ambassadors."

His answer piqued my interest. Apparently X was suffering from a condition common to journalists who are relentlessly exposed to a diet of bleak events that expose the darker side of the human character. The symptoms can take several forms. Sometimes the journalists simply burn out and quit the business. Other times they become calloused and cynical, encasing themselves in a protective shell that prevents them from feeling anything. Some become so over-sensitized to the daily barrage of cruel events that they turn moody, angry, cynical, or despondent. Chip confirmed that this latter condition described X, who felt certain that he had witnessed more evil and human stupidity in the last several years than at any other time during his career. "He has lost the ability to maintain the necessary detachment," Chip said.

Chip then recited a litany of major news events in the last several years that reflected serious problems facing the world. They ranged from bloody terrorism in the name of many causes to economic terrorism in the pursuit of wealth, among others. He said he shared X's concerns about many of these "missteps," as he called them. Other Ambassadors concurred with Chip that these missteps—what I inferred were the unfortunate results of the behaviors of that notorious 20 percent—could actually affect the timetable.

That statement certainly shocked me, but when he told me that X *was actually lobbying the Verdants to delay the event,* I was absolutely stunned.

When the Cold War ended early in the last decade, it appeared that humanity had arrived at a point where the possibility and dream of world peace was finally within reach. The Verdants and many humans shared this feeling, Chip said. The Verdants' optimism played a key role in their decision to go ahead with the planned contact and thus begin the recruitment program. Sure, Earth was still a troubled place, but the future looked promising. It was anticipated that problems would be resolved at an escalating rate and that humankind would march into the 21st century to the beat of a different drummer.

But the headlines since then have told a different story, a tale of opportunities lost and hopes unfulfilled.

"Is it possible that the human race simply is incapable of getting along?" he asked rhetorically. "Will the ancient tribal mentalities always predominate? It's almost as if there were an organized, deliberate attempt to create worldwide turmoil, to put our worst foot forward, as though this insanity is being orchestrated."

There was more. He said that some government leaders had already been briefed by Ambassadors and that one or more of them may secretly oppose the contact because of hidden personal agendas. Creating international strife, opening old wounds, instigating economic and social turmoil would be acceptable tactics that could have the desired effect of disrupting the plan, he said.

I brought the conversation back to X. Chip said that X was furious over what he perceived as a societal relapse and wanted a postponement because he believed that humans had failed to live up to expectations of the Verdants. He was very vocal in his opposition, and—because he also wielded considerable influence in certain quarters—he had gained some support from other Ambassadors.

"What we have is a small rebellion on our hands," Chip said.

That single statement alarmed me more than any other I had heard since I returned from the ship. I questioned him about the implications, about its possible effect upon the timetable. He assured me that nothing had substantially changed, although the Verdants had been listening very closely to X and reevaluating world conditions.

In my view this opposition in and of itself wasn't

enough to scuttle the program, and I believe Chip tended to agree with me. But he did add the caveat ". . . if we don't blow ourselves up first. It would be a tragedy of unparalleled proportions to miss such a golden opportunity," he said wistfully.

"So if we don't blow ourselves up, they'll be coming according to plan, according to the timetable?"

He paused and gave me a tired smile.

"What do you think?" he asked sincerely.

I was optimistic and told him so.

"So what's the bottom line?" I asked.

"The bottom line? Pray," he answered simply.

The hour was getting late, the sun was beginning to settle low in the west, and it seemed like a good time to end our conversation.

"Will I be seeing you again?" I asked.

"Let's hope that all goes according to plan, and if it does, we can share a toast sometime soon in the company of the many dedicated men and women who believe in the future," he replied. "Perhaps it will be in Genesis."

He extended his hand to me. "Goodbye, my friend." And with that he walked away.

surprise visitor

One morning, about nine months later, I was in the middle of taking a couple of loaves of banana nut bread out of the oven when the doorbell rang. It never seems to fail, I thought. I put the pans on a rack, then pulled off the hot-pad mittens and tossed them onto the counter. It was 10 a.m. on Wednesday, January 12, 2000.

At the door was a young woman, perhaps in her early 30s, attractive in a girl-next-door kind of way. She was neatly dressed in a skirt and blouse that I would guess probably came from the racks of Sears rather than Sachs. Her shoes were simple brown pumps. Her auburn hair fell in soft waves to about shoulder length, and she wore just a touch of makeup on her eyes and lips. She flashed a beguiling smile of straight, white teeth.

At first I figured her for a religious proselytizer.

"Hello," she said. She wrinkled her button nose and leaned into the doorway. "Something smells awfully good," she said.

"Yeah, I'm doing a little baking," I replied.

Several seconds passed and we merely stared at each other. The radiant smile remained on her cute face while her deep green eyes sparkled. Finally, when it seemed that she wasn't going to say anything further, I asked, "Can I help you?"

"Oh, I was just in the neighborhood and thought I'd drop by to say hi, to see how things are going," she said.

I ran her face through all of the memory banks that I could access at the moment, but drew a blank. A neighbor? A forgotten acquaintance? A friend of my wife? I simply could not place her. Perhaps she was mistaken and had come to the wrong house. I knew I wasn't going to bluff my way out—I was going to have to ask her who she was. I also knew that I probably was going to feel foolish when she told me.

"I'm afraid you have me at a disadvantage," I said cheerfully. "I don't recognize you." I hoped my squirming would go unnoticed.

"Well, I've changed a bit since we last saw each other," she said with a coy grin. "You haven't changed, of course, except that you're dressed now. The last time I saw you, you were in your underwear. You've also picked up a few pounds." She mischievously poked a finger into the little roll around my midsection.

I stared blankly at her. Brain circuits opened and closed as I searched for some familiar landmark. A pretty young woman, me in my underwear. It was a rather improbable link, but apparently there was a connection. I had recently seen a female doctor, but this certainly wasn't her.

Suddenly a light went on.

"Gina?" I asked in a husky whisper.

My God, was it really her? I was just about to throw my arms around her when my cautious nature urged me to slow down. It may be just an ordinary human female who had read my book and was engaged in a prank, I told myself. I had to think of something, some information that we had exchanged that was not in the book. But what?

Then it hit me—her real name, her Verdant name. She had told me what it was, but I had never used it. Therefore, no reader—no one on Earth, as far as I knew—had that information. And I remembered it easily for several reasons. First, it didn't contain any of those unpronounceable sounds that peppered the Verdant language. Second, it was quite a pretty name, one that I considered lyrical: Gretcheenyal (a phonetic spelling of the sound that I heard). And third, the human female name "Gina" sounded like it could be an appropriate nickname for it.

"What's your name," I asked, perhaps a little too distantly, too suspiciously.

"I'm really Gina," she replied in a sprightly voice, giving me a look of assurance.

I stared at her again. I had never really appreciated the range of expressions capable in the human face before meeting the Verdants. Whereas it took intense study and observation to finally begin to recognize the minuscule fluctuations in the facial muscles that express Verdant moods and emotions, the human face is like an open book. And right now, a look of questioning and incomprehension played across the woman's features. Then her face brightened.

"Oh, of course," she said. "I'm Gretcheenyal."

Spontaneously, I grabbed her and clutched her in a bear hug. She giggled as I planted a big kiss on her cheek. I broke away and took both of her hands in mine.

"Come in," I said, drawing her into the living room, closing the door behind her. "What are . . . how did . . . what happened . . . why are you . . . ?" This was more than a surprise; it was sheer amazement. After my visit to the ship in 1997 and the events that followed, I really believed I had lost my capacity for being amazed.

I was wrong.

"Whoa. Hold on. Slow down," she said, laughing. She was delighted by my reaction. It was written all over her expressive human face.

I took her into the kitchen, sat her down at the table, and put two enormous slices of the freshly baked and still warm bread onto plates. I set out two forks, poured us each a cup of herbal tea, then slathered each slab of bread with a generous portion of fresh creamery butter.

Between bites and sips of the tea, she told me that she had been genetically altered and beamed down only seconds before she rang the doorbell. Since I live on a cul-de-sac, which is generally quiet and deserted during the day, there was no problem in her arriving unnoticed. Besides, my "front" door is actually on the side of the house and is largely hidden from street view.

(I recall Gina saying upon her arrival that she had been genetically altered, but my notes are not crystal clear about this. I'm going to assume she was, as I was directly told on my first visit to the ship in 1997 that the Verdants had mastered this process. It has been suggested to me that her appearance might have been a mental or holographic projection of some sort, which I would not rule out. However, this seems unlikely because, as you will now see, she maintained her form during our stroll through a local mall, and in fact was noticed by others there as we walked and talked.)

As I gazed fondly at her delicate features, I was suddenly overcome with a sense of deja vu. The memory of a dream came rushing back to my consciousness, and I excitedly shared with her my recollection.

"C'mon, fess up, now," she said. "You've had many revealing and insightful dreams, haven't you? That certainly wasn't the only one."

She was right, of course. I had started to dream in volumes, and they began taking on such form and substance that I wondered if they were more than mere nighttime fantasies, if they might possibly have been some form of communication. There was an interesting pattern in the way they played out, almost like one of the old movie serials of yore. In the first installment, Gina visited me in human form and told me that I would return to the ship. After three or four such dreams, it became obvious that they were all part of a continuing saga; each one picked up where the preceding one left off. It was like a story falling into place, and I began looking forward to sleeping each night and to whatever new surprises and revelations the next installment might bring.

The nocturnal sagas continued sporadically over a period of months until I had a complete story, with a very definite beginning in which I was prepared for a return to the ship, a middle in which I was back among the aliens and was continuing my education, and an end in which I bade farewell to my hosts and returned to my home.

I finally asked her if the Verdants had been contacting me while I slept.

"This bread is wonderful," she said as she washed the last of it down with a gulp of tea. "I wouldn't be able to eat it in my Verdant form, though."

She must have had a good reason to avoid my question so I decided to play along. But I was absolutely determined that I was going to get some answers before she left the house.

"Why not?" I asked. "There's no meat in it."

"I know, but Verdants can't digest butter or any other animal by-products," she replied. "Our bodies aren't equipped to process anything but plant matter. It's just a matter of simple physiology."

I mentioned that the bread also contained eggs and milk, but she said that was no problem in her human form. Even meat could be digested in her present biological configuration, but consuming flesh would not be considered because of moral objections. Even if the Verdants had the digestive systems to process meat, they would never do so.

"Anyway," I said, "I know you didn't travel 250,000 miles to compliment me on my cooking. First, I'd like you to answer my question about the dreams. Then I want to know why you're here. Do you have good news for me?"

To me, good news would be that I would be going back

to the *Goodwill*. While the events being played out now were not identical to the dream that I had along these lines, there were striking similarities in some areas.

"OK, the dreams. Yes, we were in contact with your subconscious mind for reasons that you wouldn't understand even if I explained them to you. Let's just say that we have our methodologies, our procedures, our agendas. They serve a purpose for us, but you shouldn't put too much stock in them. Certainly you shouldn't interpret them literally. That's the best advice I can give you," she said.

She picked at the few remaining crumbs on her plate, wetting a finger to snag them and then licking it. I offered her another slice, but she declined.

"It's very good, but I'm stuffed," she said. After a pause, she continued. "Yes, I have good news for you, if you consider an invitation to return to the ship as good news."

I could not restrain my excitement. It was something that I had been hoping for and that had occupied my mind for much of the previous two years. I beamed a broad, elated smile, jumped up from my chair in a moment of unbridled enthusiasm, grabbed one of her hands in both of mine and shook it enthusiastically.

What the heck, I thought. In a moment of sheer joy in which I threw decorum to the wind, I pulled her to me and hugged her. Her hair had a wonderfully clean smell. This figure before me was for the moment not an alien but a lovely human woman, and as I held her tightly to me, feeling the shapely waist beneath the arm that I had wrapped tightly around it, I suddenly experienced a reaction that went beyond mere friendship.

I turned her loose and quickly stepped back. An

embrace that began as an expression of delight and enthusiasm had quickly escalated into something inappropriate.

Gina gave me a coquettish grin and took her chair again.

"My, my. Were you being naughty?" she asked.

I actually blushed. Even at my grandfatherly age, I could feel the heat of my reddening cheeks as though I were some awkward schoolboy.

"I'm sorry," I whispered. "That took me totally by surprise, and I meant no disrespect."

Gina chuckled and waved off my uneasy apology with a flip of her arm that said I was making too much of it.

Odd as it may sound, Gina and I had had a previous "sexual history." On my first visit to the alien spacecraft in 1997, Gina and I found ourselves alone in a lounge area during one of the informal periods in which she was showing me around the ship. She had been asking very pointed questions about the mating habits of humans, a subject that made me somewhat uncomfortable, and I kept trying to steer the conversation in other directions.

But she had persisted, and eventually exposed her naked body to me and suggested a sexual encounter, which I immediately spurned. It was obvious to me at the time that she was not driven by any particular passion for me but rather by simple curiosity. The Verdants have a healthy open attitude about sex and do not burden the subject with the kind of moral, spiritual, and emotional baggage with which some humans tend to overload it.

She had not been offended by my rejection, and that

was the end of the matter. I wrote about that incident—and one other with heavy religious and spiritual overtones—in detail in *The Contact Has Begun,* although my initial inclination was to omit both. The sexual episode was embarrassing to me and I felt awkward and uneasy about relating it. (Was this an example of the emotional "baggage" that we humans attach to the subject of sex—in this case prudery?) My report about the spiritual incident was also extremely controversial, and to compound the difficulty, I felt inadequate about writing on this subject because of my woeful lack of knowledge about even the fundamentals of religion.

Since neither incident was integral to the construction of the white paper, I felt justified in leaving them out. But after much agonizing, I felt that I should include them as a matter of accurately recording all events in order to give the complete story of what had occurred during my three days aboard the ship. It was a decision that was destined to get me into a bit of hot water, as you will see later in this book.

"Come on, we've got some work to do," Gina said to me in my kitchen.

And so we settled back down to business.

"I said there was good news," Gina continued. "And while there is no conversely bad news as such, I do want you to be aware that there is a serious side to the purpose of the invitation. In other words, your return will not be a mere lark but involves matters of genuine concern with sobering implications."

What in the world did that mean? She explained that all Ambassadors were being recalled for short work sessions and mini-conferences to iron out some difficulties that had arisen and to address some deep questions that had surfaced over the previous year. Most of the Ambassadors had already been debriefed, some were currently in the process of being so, and a very small number still had yet to be recalled. Only a very select few of the Deputy Envoys—of which I was one—would actually make the return trip to the ship. The remainder would be briefed in other ways.

Her face and voice had taken on a more serious bearing. I asked her if anything was wrong.

"Nothing to become overly alarmed about." She put a cheerful look on her face. "Let's leave it at that for the time being."

"Can we take a tour?" she asked. "I'd like to see your neighborhood. I've never been on Earth before."

"Sure," I said. "Do you want to walk or take a drive?"

"Let's drive," she replied.

Making sure she was buckled up, I backed the car out of the garage and took her to the grocery store down the street. At the store she wandered the aisles in fascination for about half an hour. Undoubtedly, the store was primitive by her standards, but even we humans can find enchantment in poking around in the ruins of ancient civilizations. Then we headed for the local mall, and it was immediately obvious from the moment we set foot inside that she could be there until closing time. She was enthralled as we roamed each store in consecutive order.

We talked as we walked. It was simple chitchat, nothing at all to do with momentous events of the past or those still to come. Instead of asking the price of various items that caught her eye, she asked me how many hours or days an average person would have to work to pay for them. There was no easy answer because such questions then led us into discussions about the distribution of wealth under our system. I had to explain that a doctor might have to work only an hour or so to buy a sport coat or a fancy tie, while a bank teller or a laborer might have to work several days to earn the price of the same item.

At one point we stopped at the food court. I purchased an order of rice for her from a Chinese fast-food outlet, and for myself chose a slice of plain cheese pizza from another restaurant. I had deliberately selected the rice in an effort to avoid anything containing animal products.

She took one taste of the rice and immediately spit it out. The look of distress on her face shocked me. Apparently it had been prepared with a small amount of chicken stock, which she immediately detected. I tasted it myself and just couldn't tell. We continued our tour, and so the day went.

"When can I go back?" I eventually asked.

"We've made arrangements for Saturday afternoon. Monday is a holiday in much of your nation so we'll have a few others there also. It's a good time for them to get away."

I stopped on the spot and turned to face her. A couple behind me almost ran into us. The man muttered something under his breath as they passed.

"You bet," I said. "I'll be ready. It's a date."

I then told her of a dream I had had in the middle of one week in which I was told that I would go back to the ship on the following Saturday. This dream had occurred during a period when I was attempting to make telepathic communication with the Verdants and had entertained the seemingly bizarre notion that they might be communicating with me in my dreams. After I awoke that morning, I wasn't sure whether my dream was just a common, ordinary nocturnal fantasy or whether they had actually contacted me in my sleep. Nevertheless, I counted down the days to the weekend.

The eagerly anticipated Saturday came and went uneventfully, I told her.

Gina smiled and winked at me.

We roamed the mall for another couple of hours and then headed back to the house. It was nearly 6 p.m., and my wife would soon be getting home from work. Gina said that my wife was welcome to accompany me and that she would like to meet her. I promised to pass along the invitation.

I parked the car, closed the garage door with the remote, and invited her back into the house. She declined and said she needed to leave but that she would see me on Saturday.

"If your wife decides to come along, just hold her hand at that time and we'll know," she said.

She pulled a small device from the pocket of her skirt, and almost instantly the inside of the garage—including me—was bathed in the familiar bluish-white light.

The light narrowed into a beam focused upon her.

"Until Saturday, then," she said, and disappeared along with the light.

reunion

After Gina returned to her ship, I jumped onto the computer and began typing furiously. Mostly I typed dialogue while our conversations were still fresh in my mind. It was 4 a.m. before I finally quit and crawled into bed, exhausted. Despite my lack of sleep, I got up at 8 a.m. when I heard my wife stirring. I hadn't told her about the visit the evening before because I wanted to devote my full time to getting the notes into the computer.

But now I was anxious to tell her about the incident before I sat down in front of the computer again. I could barely contain myself as I breathlessly blurted out the events of the day before.

As I suspected, she showed little enthusiasm for discussing my experience and declined the invitation to join me in returning to the ship. It was clearly a difficult issue for her, and I asked if she thought I was crazy, had imagined the whole thing, was cracking up.

She sighed deeply. "No, I'm just nervous about the whole thing, so it's easier to not talk about it. I like our lives the way they are. I don't want things to change."

She smiled.

"If you were cracking up, as you put it, sometimes I think that might be easier to handle."

Thursday and Friday passed uneventfully, with my wife going off to work while I finished my typing. The night before my departure, though, she got up several times, so I knew that she wasn't sleeping well. The next morning we settled into our daily ritual: I read the newspaper while she sipped her coffee.

"You said sometime in the afternoon?" she asked after a time.

Not only had my wife declined the invitation to go, but she announced plans to take off for a few days to visit friends out of town. She didn't even want to see me off. I was agreeable to that. She packed a bag about noon and took off in the car.

One of the most frequently asked questions concerns how my wife deals with my experience. I think it can be summed up in the following exchange between her and an acquaintance that I overheard one day.

"I read your husband's book. Did that really happen?"

"Not to me," my wife replied.

"What was it like?"

"You're asking the wrong person," my wife said.

"I guess you don't want to talk about it."

"It's not my story. If you have questions, ask my husband."

I went about my usual business during the day, staying inside the house at all times. I made sure that I was wearing more than my underwear this time and slipped into a sweat suit. I also retrieved from my files a packet of letters and e-mail messages from readers who had offered their services in support of the program for contact. Whenever I received such communications, I would tell aspiring volunteers that I had no voice in the selection process but would give their letters to the proper authorities if the opportunity came up. It looked as though I was finally going to be able to fulfill that promise.

I also made sure that I had my reading glasses, then decided not to take any cigarettes. I never once had a craving for a smoke during my first time aboard, and the Verdants would not have allowed me to light up anyway.

Since I didn't know how long I would have to wait, I propped myself up in my bed at about two o'clock and surfed the TV.

A couple of hours later, the familiar bluish-white light suddenly filled the room. My heart was thumping rapidly, but it was from excitement and not apprehension or fear. The beam focused narrowly upon me, and the next thing I knew I was in a small room, much smaller than the cavernous examination hall that had greeted me during my first visit. Two of the familiar disks from which the beams of light emanated were attached to the ceiling.

There was nothing particularly unique or special about the room, nothing that would make it stand out from what I had observed on my first visit aboard. The wall, ceiling, and floor colors were the usual neutral variety, what we humans would call earth tones. The temperature was comfortable, about 70 degrees Fahrenheit, and a couple of the ubiquitous lounge chairs sat against one wall. As usual, there were no paintings on the walls, no vases of flowers or plants to dress it up. The best description would be semibarren utilitarian.

Much to my surprise, I immediately recognized Gus (who had been assigned to me on my first visit). Gina, whose subtle features I had come to know, was there as well. I was making continuing progress in learning to make the fine distinctions necessary to distinguish between individual Verdants. Four other Verdants were also in the room.

Gus uncharacteristically reached out and shook my hand and, if I was correctly reading the almost imperceptible signs of emotion on his face, seemed pleased to see me again. I gave Gina a light embrace.

"You've changed," I said with a grin in reference to the human form in which I had last seen her.

One of the other Verdants in the group handed me a robe and a pair of slippers, which I held awkwardly for a few moments before Gus finally spoke up.

"We've seen you in your underwear before, but if you want some privacy to change, that can be arranged."

I felt remarkably unselfconscious, so I put on the robe and slippers after stepping out of my clothes. I thanked the Verdant who had handed me the garments, but wasn't quite sure of what to do with the sheaf of letters and the eyeglass case, which I was still holding. I considered stuffing the papers inside the robe against my chest but that still left the matter of the glasses.

"What's this?" Gus asked, pointing to the papers.

"These are letters and notes from readers who have volunteered their services to help with the transition," I explained. "Most of the writers are very enthusiastic about wanting to play an active role. Some of the letters are from people who want to be Ambassadors or Deputy Envoys. And there are several from people who want to apply for jobs. A few resumes are included, and some of them are pretty impressive."

"How generous," Gus said as he reached for the packet, which I surrendered. He in turn handed them to one of the other four Verdants. Gus spoke some words in that incomprehensible language of theirs, and the Verdant who now had the letters turned and left the room.

"They'll be entered into the record," he said.

I thanked him. Without any prompting on my part, he reached for my eyeglass case and brushed it down along the left sleeve of his robe from shoulder to elbow, then placed it against my own robe over the left breast. Amazingly, it adhered snugly. Out of curiosity, I reached for the case and pulled it free of the robe. It came off easily, as though it had been attached by Velcro, but there was no visible connecting tissue. It was almost as if it were being held magnetically.

The familiar name tags were in evidence all about me. They generally tipped me off to gender because the females typically take feminine names used on Earth, and the males take masculine ones. There was an occasional Pat or Marty, but that wasn't a problem because I had learned that the males are taller than the females and not quite as slightly built. The females also had typically feminine physiques, though less pronounced than they are on Earth, more like adolescent bodies though I knew that many of them were probably thousands of years old!

"We have a little surprise for you," Gus said. He and Gina led me a couple of doors down from the room we were in through a nondescript corridor.

The other Verdants stayed behind. To my surprise, I soon found myself entering a large reception room that was filled with about a dozen humans, presumably Ambassadors.

The setting was more festive than the normally rather austere Verdant style. Around the perimeter of the room were a number of tables that could seat four people each, and one long table covered with an ornate white tablecloth on which a wide variety of platters of food and drink rested. Some of the morsels rested in crinkled little paper cups in various pastel shades, typical of the colors that the Verdants seemed to prefer. None of the drinks were alcoholic, although they were tantalizingly delicious.

"Human" music played in the background. During the course of the "evening," I recognized some old standards, a country/Western tune or two, some catchy rock' n' roll of the Buddy Holly and Elvis Presley variety, and a few stately waltzes. With the exception of rap or hip-hop—which I personally abhor and consider emblematic of the cultural rot that I see spreading across the body of America—the music was an eclectic mix that spanned several generations. It seemed to emanate from everywhere and nowhere, yet never became intrusive.

"Enjoy yourself. Get to know the others," Gus said. "We'll talk later." He and Gina then walked out the door, leaving the room occupied only by humans.

During the course of this unusual evening, I met and spoke with everyone who was there. They all wore name tags, but I was sure even then that most, if not all, of the names were assumed. The only people I recognized were Chip and Paul, the two people I had met nearly a year earlier near San Francisco, but they too were probably using pseudonyms.

Initially, I was surprised when I caught sight of Chip sitting at a table with a couple of other people. I shouldn't have been, because what could be more natural than to find him in this setting. I finally caught his eye, and he beamed and waved me over. We shook hands warmly.

He introduced me to Carl and Lorraine, husband and wife. Most of the guests during the course of the gathering refrained from talking business or revealing anything but the barest personal information about themselves. On the basis of a few less-than-telltale comments, I guessed that Carl might be a political scientist, perhaps a professor at a university. Mystery-man Paul soon joined our group as well.

As I mingled and chatted, enjoying the mood and the savory food, I introduced myself to Beverly, a matronly type who was there with her husband, Hal. I got the impression that both were active in the UFO community and belonged to several organizations. I sized up a beefy man called Jim as possibly a law enforcement officer with a degree in sociology. Although I refer to him as beefy, I'm trying to keep physical descriptions of the guests to a minimum so as not to compromise anyone's identity. In general, there seemed to be a representative mix of race and gender.

I thought that Megan, a beautiful woman in her mid-30s, might be an educator although even if that assessment is correct, it could mean anything from an elementary school teacher to the dean of a university. During the course of the evening she made several impassioned comments about the current state of public education, including what she considered a lack of adequate public support for the schools, the poor condition of many campuses, and violence in schoolyards.

Then there was Tony, mid-40s, handsome. He was divorced, but never mentioned anything about having children. I pegged him as a government official of some sort, but my supposition was based only on one scant comment in which he worried that some governments might be riddled with people with a vested interest opposed to the contact.

A couple named Mary and Tom were two of the more interesting guests, and although I think I have a good idea about their occupations, I'm not going to publicly speculate. If I'm even close, the combination would be so distinctive that revealing it could have the effect of narrowing down a guess about their identities from millions of people to perhaps a dozen or so. This much I learned and don't have to speculate about: Both are extremely well-educated and Tom was once a military pilot. They put a lot of store in the social graces and, while not prudes, believe that good manners and civility are deteriorating in human society. I had no idea at that time whether both of them were official emissaries.

Lillian, the last of the group I mention, revealed little

about herself except to say that she was divorced, had two grown children, and was seeing someone.

That was it: 13 of us gathered together in a single room miles above Earth's surface, chewing the fat and socializing, much as we would at a hometown cocktail party (without the cocktails).

At first I had the impression that none of us had an inkling about the purpose of our recall but that we were nevertheless certain that we would learn about it quite soon. But as the hours wore on, I gathered that the others knew precisely why they were there. In fact, it seems that I was the only one who was still in the dark. Gina had been evasive about the purpose of my return, saying only that some meetings would be held to iron out a number of issues or problems that had arisen. Although she had said that there were some serious concerns, I assumed that such matters were of a more routine than calamitous nature, considering the immensity of the undertaking. Planning something the size of an intergalactic and interspecies summit conference certainly was bound to bring complications, and that's what I thought we were going to be dealing with.

It was impossible to pick up any substantive insights, though with every bit of information I could glean, my curiosity grew. People just weren't divulging anything but the most meager and insubstantial facts about themselves; protocol and simple courtesy dictated that I refrain from asking deeper personal questions.

"You know that you're the only one here who has his real name on his name tag, don't you?" Jim asked me at one point as he chewed on what appeared to be barbecued ribs. They were, of course, plant material and not real meat.

Those who have read my first book will recall that on my first visit to the ship, I was served a wide variety of foods that would appeal to the most sophisticated palate, only to learn that all of it was synthesized from one particular plant that is the mainstay of the Verdant diet. That included what appeared to be "meat" as well as all other artificial animal products such as the Verdant rendition of eggs, milk, cheese, etc. Verdants not only eschew meat on moral and ethical grounds, but also are biologically incapable of digesting flesh. The moral prohibition does not extend to animal products that can be gathered with no harm to the animal donor, such as eggs and milk—and by-products such as cheese and yogurt—but even these are indigestible. As such, Verdants are strict vegetarians.

I replied that I had gathered as much. Jim also told me that I was the only one among the group whose identity was known by all of the others.

"So, you don't know everybody here?" I asked.

"I don't know anybody here," he said, sweeping the room with a hand that held a chunk of ribs. "Nobody knows anybody else."

Either he was mistaken or he wasn't being completely open. I knew for a fact that Paul and Chip were, at the least, acquaintances. They might even have been good friends. But I saw no point in making an issue of the matter, and I let it slide. I figured they all had to know me because of my first book.

"The only one we know is you," Jim continued. "But the night is young yet, and some people might get to know each other a bit better, get to learn something about the other. There's no rule against it."

Then he gave me a wink and a nudge as he rolled his eyes and head in the direction of a table where Tony and Megan were engaged in what appeared to be intimate conversation. They were holding hands.

"They seem to have hit it off pretty well." His grin would have to be described as lascivious.

As soon as I could tactfully do so, I steered the conversation onto other subjects. I knew that I would learn soon enough the purpose of this recall in general and, specifically, how it affected me. But it was difficult to contain my curiosity.

Perhaps if the Verdants had seen fit to serve cocktails, the alcohol might have oiled some tongues. All of them seemed to be in complete control of their faculties, however, and so my little fishing expedition yielded little more than nibbles. About the only thing I learned from Jim was that there were at the time of our conversation exactly 873 Ambassadors currently active. Several of those were backup, because a few had died. In a few cases, several Ambassadors had dropped out for one reason or another, mostly because of stress.

It didn't strike me as particularly important at the time, but I also learned that every one of the currently active Ambassadors had already been back aboard the ship for this recall and that the group that was now here represented the final contingent. That little bit of news should have pricked my ears, but its significance escaped me at the time, and it wouldn't be until much later that the full import of it finally became obvious.

I also learned that there were 822 Deputy Envoys, although only a few of them had been brought back aboard for this recall program. Because the vast majority would not be playing critical roles in the contact, no crucial problem would result from any deaths or dropouts among their ranks. Besides, they were easier to replace.

That was all of the information of any consequence that I could wring out of Jim, unless one considers details of his sexual exploits of any particular interest, or his philosophy with respect to open marriages and sexual freedom. I really had no interest in these matters, but I listened politely while waiting for the slightest opening to excuse myself and seek out other company.

Even when modest Lillian came up to us carrying a little plate with a variety of dainty snacks, Jim felt no reservations about continuing his frank and personal discourse, to which she took certain strong exceptions, particularly with respect to the sanctity of marriage.

They got involved in a heated debate, each arguing his and her point of view with passion. At one point, I thought that Lillian might even slap Jim's face, especially when he brought up the fact that she was divorced to make one of his raw points. I gazed about the room, hoping to catch someone's eye so that I could break away without appearing artless.

"Civilized behavior is what separates us from the beasts of the world. There are rules, moral and religious values—both on a group and personal level—ethical considerations of fidelity, love, and trust embodied in the marriage bonds," she argued.

She accused him of being no different from an animal in the wild.

He countered that throughout history, rich and powerful men—the patriarchs—invariably had concubines, mistresses, and even multiple wives. Less influential men—the plebeians—didn't have the same opportunities. Nevertheless, he opined, even though there are no groupies for mechanics and carpenters (and here he burst out laughing at his droll observation), the average man also dabbles, although he usually has to settle for prostitutes, bar pickups, one-night stands, and office affairs that often end messily. Monogamy, he said, is not a natural state for a sexual being.

"Oh, I don't know," I interjected, not really wanting to get into the conversation but unable to resist responding to such a provocative statement. "My marriage is solid and is quite comfortable for me."

"Thank you," Lillian said, grateful for the support. "Marriage and family are the cornerstones of civilized societies in virtually every culture."

"Well, there's an old folk saying," Jim finally conceded. "Kisses wear out, cooking don't."

I guess that was supposed to have some meaning, but it escaped me.

Paradoxically, despite the outward displays of seeming hostility, I got the impression that secretly they were engaged in a little game and were actually enjoying the interplay. It might even be described as flirtatious, but I was finding it tiresome. Sometimes I wonder if anyone really understands the full depth of human sexuality.

I finally was able to excuse myself, and wandered off toward Mary and Tom, who were engaged in conversation with Paul. Perhaps it was my imagination, but they seemed to change the subject as I came closer. I had caught Mary's eye as I was heading in their direction, and it was apparent

ch 3   reunion   47

that she had mentioned my approach to the others, because she broke eye contact and whispered something to the other two, who quickly gave me sidelong glances.

I asked if I was interrupting, but was assured that they weren't speaking of anything of consequence.

"Does anybody have any idea why we're here?" I asked, surprised at my own frankness. I had been playing it cool and casual all "evening," trying not to pry into areas where it appeared that barriers had been erected, but I was getting frustrated. While all of the guests that I spoke to had been friendly and respectful, I got the definite impression that they knew something that I didn't and weren't about to share it with me. (I would learn later that issues of momentous import having a direct bearing upon my fate were going to be discussed during the conferences and that everyone I had met knew this.)

Even the responses that I got in this group weren't helpful, as though each person was walking a fine line between telling me an outright lie and fudging answers in such a way as to appear that they were responding. I simply could find nothing in their eloquently expressed words to provide me with any new insights. I decided to change the subject.

"So, Paul, what have you been up to since the last time we met?" I asked.

"Oh, I've been keeping busy," he responded with a smile.

"You two have met before?" Mary asked. "I was under the impression that we were all strangers to each other. Of course, we all know who you are because you have gone public."

"None of us has gone public yet," Tom added. "Hopefully, it won't be too much longer before we can start coming out and joining you."

I briefly explained that I had met Paul—and Chip—nearly a year earlier. This revelation raised Mary's and Tom's eyebrows, and they said they hadn't been aware of that. I said that it was no secret, because I had already revealed it, although it didn't get much public attention. I had written a manuscript called *The Verdant Agenda,* which was an update on events that had occurred after the publication of *The Contact Has Begun.* I had posted it on a popular Internet web site in late 1999 and left it there for about a month before I pulled it.

(Because it dealt with predictions that had been made during the rendezvous in Pinole, I wanted to go on record before the end of the year and the start of the new millennium. That way, no one could accuse me of writing those predictions after the fact. It served that purpose.)

For a brief moment I thought about my discussions with Paul and Chip that day, much of which were shared in chapter 1. That afternoon had seemed a privileged time, a special time; the experience was one I will never forget. Yet here I now was, somehow on the outside looking in, and it didn't feel special at all despite my being back on the ship.

. . . I was brought out of my self-absorption when I heard Paul say, "Tom and Mary were explaining to me that they don't believe in the American jury system."

"Really?" I responded. "Why not?"

The couple took turns expressing their points of views, sometimes even finishing sentences for one another. They said they didn't want to be perceived as snobbish or elitist, but pointed out that the people in this gathering (I exclude myself from this observation) were without exception all on the high end of the intelligence scale. Some of them might even be characterized as geniuses, they said.

"And the point is?" I asked.

"How many people in this room do you think ever served on a jury?" Tom asked.

I had no idea. Personally, I'd shown up for jury duty on two occasions, but had never been selected as a juror.

"Juries are made up of 12 people randomly picked off the street," he explained. "How in blazes are 12 average people—at least one would have to be a moron based on the law of averages—supposed to rule intelligently on highly complex laws and pieces of evidence that even the educated, highly skilled, experienced lawyers and judges can't agree on?"

"Let's take a survey," Mary said enthusiastically. "This should be fun!"

So we went around the room in a group and polled the others. The result: none. I was the only exception.

That proved their point, Tom and Mary said. Their argument was that highly intelligent people generally are too involved in more important matters to be inclined to spend hours, days, or weeks in discussions with a random bunch of average people trying to decide if some fool is guilty of drunk driving or a second-rate burglary. But the most frustrating and unrewarding part of such duty, they declared, is the maddening realization that many of the other jurors simply aren't equipped to do critical thinking, and so the reasoned arguments of the intelligent simply fall on deaf ears.

I was going to say something about civic responsibility

but decided not to get further involved. I wondered if the discussions I had heard so far were typical of the exchanges that take place whenever academics and intellectuals get together. For the most part they struck me as surprisingly supercilious and pompous.

I glanced at Paul who seemed to be listening indifferently, contributing nothing of substance to the discussion.

"Jurors are retirees—and office workers, mail carriers, low-level government workers," Tom said.

"And gardeners, factory workers, housewives," Mary chimed in.

"Newspaper reporters and editors," Tom continued, "but not high-level editors."

"Touché," I said with mock grace.

"Mechanics, auto sales people, truck drivers," Mary continued.

"Your average guy on the street. Not highly intelligent people with important jobs and powerful positions," Tom said. "Anybody can get out of jury duty. It's simple. But the people who serve on juries do so because they want to. It gets them away from their dreary, humdrum jobs. It spices up their tedious lives, gives them something to talk about, makes them feel important, gives some of them a sense of power and worth. Mostly they're pathetic."

"Thank you for sharing that with me," I said with just enough sarcasm to make my point without being brusque. I excused myself and walked away. I may not be the sharpest guy in the world, but the idea that I probably had little in common with most of these people was beginning to become evident.

I respect and admire intellect, and one of the pleasures that I derived from my 25-year career at the *Times* was coming into contact on a daily basis with some remarkably intelligent and creative people. While most of them were as affable and easygoing as the next guy, a few of them were royal pains in the neck. They were blessed with extraordinary cerebral talents, and they knew it, but they lacked the requisite character traits and social skills to keep their uniqueness in perspective when interacting with others who were less gifted. That is, they could be overbearing prima donnas.

The plain truth is, special people are still just that—people—and they have all of the foibles, peccadilloes, failings, and drawbacks that define us as a species. There's no doubt that these people by and large are my betters, but that doesn't excuse gratuitous incivility and insolence.

I stopped at the food table and helped myself to a cup of fruit punch of some sort and a couple of finger sandwiches. As I gazed casually around the room, my eye landed on a table where Hal and Beverly had been talking with Lorraine, who at that moment was getting up to join her husband.

"Mind if I sit down?" I asked, setting my cup and plate on the table.

They both smiled and graciously offered me a seat. We talked for about half an hour about nothing in particular until I casually made a reference to some item in my book. I knew the subject was practically *verboten* because I had already recognized the pattern; the conversation would inevitably be steered in another direction whenever it appeared to go deeper than a mere cursory mention of the book. About the most that I could get out of anyone was simply an acknowledgment that they knew it existed and that I was the author; not one person had ventured an opinion or an observation about it.

I felt the same thing happening here, and decided to go further.

"So, what did you think of the book?" I boldly asked.

They exchanged glances; neither of them met my eyes. Hal busied himself by pretending to fish a speck of something out of his drink cup with an index finger. I wasn't fooled. There was nothing in that cup except his drink. Beverly examined her well-manicured nails.

"It was . . . interesting," Hal said, still toying with his cup. "Lots of people I know told me that they thought it was quite interesting."

"I thought so, too," Beverly said. "Yes, indeed, quite interesting."

There was an awkward silence.

"Yes, indeed, very interesting," Beverly repeated.

"And very few misspellings," Hal piped up, finally raising his eyes from the table to meet mine.

"I don't think I caught any misspellings," Beverly said charitably. Perhaps she expected me to rejoice over that rave review. "There was one sentence that had a missing word. I read it several times—that sentence, I mean—because it seemed a bit garbled. But then I realized that a word was missing; I forget exactly what. But it was just a minor thing."

"Yeah, no big deal," Hal said.

The conversation was getting so uncomfortable that I decided to change the subject myself.

I learned that it was no coincidence that none of the

guests here knew any of the other visitors, Paul and Chip being exceptions. Apparently, Beverly and Hal told me, the Verdants exercised great caution when compiling the groups to ensure that anonymity would be protected. That is, no Ambassadors had to worry about suddenly coming face-to-face with someone who knew their identity but not their relationship with the Verdants. But even as they were telling me this, I detected a hole in their reasoning the size of a crater. How in the world could some famous person—an astronaut, a movie star, a prominent public figure from any field—take part in these gatherings and not be recognized? It didn't make sense. Anonymity wasn't possible under those circumstances.

Beverly explained that the famous and the nameless are never mixed, except in cases where two or more individuals have previously met as Ambassadors. Those who are unknown—and I don't know how large that segment is—meet only with others who have no public persona. She also said that the unknowns do meet in larger groups, up to 20 at a time. Well-known Ambassadors meet only with other prominent ones and also in much smaller groups, usually about two or three at a time. In certain cases, she pointed out, some of the highest-ranking Ambassadors meet alone with the Verdants, with no other humans in attendance.

"I met a very important man during my first visit aboard," I said in rebuttal. I wasn't looking for an argument, just stating a known fact, and I was curious as to how Beverly and Hal might explain that anomaly, or what might be described as a security breach.

Both professed puzzlement about that episode, which I had described in the book, and they admitted that they were hard-pressed to come up with a reasonable explanation. I could feel the air fill with tension again as the conversation shifted from superficial to stickier subjects.

The book was obviously a touchy subject that people seemed intent on avoiding, and since we were discussing it now, I expected one of them to start talking about something else. Yet their discomfort seemed to mask a stronger desire to go on. On the one hand they wanted to drop the subject, but I could tell by the grim set of their faces and the stiffness of their manner that something inside them was bursting to be said. And then it happened.

"Maybe seeing the person on board was a test of some sort," Beverly said a bit too sweetly.

"And maybe it didn't happen," Hal said bluntly.

It took a moment for the full impact of his statement to sink in. If I wasn't mistaken, this guy was questioning my credibility. I fought to control my indignation.

"Excuse me?" I inquired icily.

"Well, what I mean is . . . meant to say . . . perhaps the man . . . ."

"He means that maybe it was just a test and that the memory was actually planted just to see what you would do with it," she said, smiling pleasantly and patting her husband's hand.

I guess it's possible that I took the statement too personally when it wasn't really intended as an assault, but there was no point in staying. The mood had definitely soured. I spent the rest of the so-called evening—at least it was evening at home—being as sociable as I could, but mostly I kept to myself.

A personal tour guide and attendant had been assigned

to each couple and individual. Six hours after I had arrived, they entered the room together and announced that it was time to return to our quarters; we had a "busy day" tomorrow. I was delighted to learn that Gina had again been assigned to me, and I was even more pleased—flattered, actually—when I learned that she had requested that assignment.

I said goodnight to the other guests, shook a few hands as we were all departing, and then accompanied Gina to my quarters. I don't know if it was the same room that I had stayed in during my first visit aboard, but it was certainly identical to it. Gina offered to have some food delivered, but I wasn't hungry.

She took her leave, I settled into the bed, and was soon sound asleep, too exhausted by the ordeal I had just gone through to worry about what lay ahead.

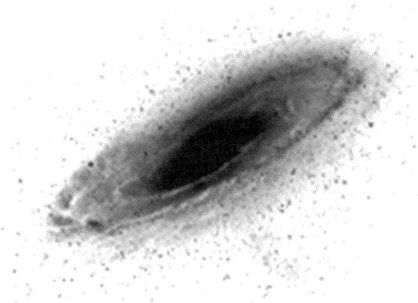

serious business

I awoke naturally and figured that the time was somewhere between 7 and 8 a.m. at home. I used what the Verdants referred to in my first book as the "comfort station," a modern affair of modest proportions that held a vanity with washbasin and drawers. There was a toilet, a shower stall, a toilet paper roll, a towel bar with clean, fresh towels. There was also a standard medicine cabinet.

I changed into some fresh clothes, and had barely stepped out of the bathroom when there came a tapping at my door. As I learned to do upon my first visit, I directed an intention toward the door, and the door responded, sliding open.

(As I explained in my previous book, Verdant doors are obviously much more sophisticated than the devices on Earth that open when someone gets close enough to activate a proximity sensor. I saw many instances on the ship where crew members would actually lean against a door, or pass within inches of one, without activating it. But once one of the aliens decided that it was going to enter or leave, the door seemed to recognize that intent and would activate, sliding into the bulkhead and then closing when the ingress or egress was completed.)

Gina walked in, followed by a male Verdant wheeling in a breakfast cart. I couldn't believe my eyes as I stared at the wide variety of hot and cold foods heaped upon it. I helped myself to small portions because I wanted to sample as much variety as I was able to handle: a dollop of scrambled eggs, one sausage link, a slice of crisp bacon, a silver-dollar pancake covered with a pat of butter and pure maple syrup, a big glass of fresh orange juice, half a cup of oatmeal with brown sugar and fresh cream and sprinkled with nutmeg. I sat at the reading table and devoured my meal while Gina sat on the edge of the bed. The male Verdant had taken his leave as soon as the table was prepared.

"What's on the agenda for today?" I asked between mouthfuls. As usual, the food was sheer ambrosia. Plant matter is grown aboard the ship hydroponically, is processed through some mysterious method, and can be preserved indefinitely. The material is then processed into an endless variety of dishes and tailored to the palates of any species whose physiology can utilize plant material as food.

She had previously assured me during her visit to my

home that while there were serious questions to be addressed and difficulties to be ironed out regarding the scheduled contact, they weren't matters that I should be concerned about. Nonetheless, I was anxious to find out what those issues were. Also, I was still troubled by the previous night; I didn't like feeling excluded, or sensing that others knew more than I did about my own involvement in the project. I was trying to keep my anxiety in check, telling myself that most likely the final plans were being laid and that we were about to get our final marching orders in preparation for the big day.

Gina explained that all of the guests at last night's reception—including the married couples—were Ambassadors, highly educated and extremely skilled in their professional fields. They would be meeting as a group with a select assembly of Verdants to present reports, offer suggestions and opinions, and provide counsel upon which important decisions would be based.

I winced when she suggested that the matters to be discussed would be so esoteric and complex that most likely I wouldn't be able to follow them, but I'm realistic enough to recognize my own intellectual and educational shortcomings. Anyway, I had no reason to doubt her assessment, and in fact was far more curious to know about the purpose of my own presence. If I wasn't going to participate in the meetings, then why had I been brought aboard?

As the food cart was being removed, another Verdant entered. His name tag said Martin. Gina introduced us.

"Martin has been designated to brief you in general terms about the nature of the proceedings that have been going on for the last few months, and to assure you that there is a purpose for your being aboard. I'll stay with you at all times," she said.

We had developed a bond and I felt confident and at ease in her presence. Call it moral support, I guess. I didn't know what Martin was up to, but having Gina at my side gave me comfort.

"Let's take a walk," Martin said, and the three of us left the room and strolled a short distance to a small transporter room where we were beamed to an intimate lounge area. The description of the teleportation process in my first book bears repeating. One feels no sensation of being transported, although that's exactly what happens. It is as though the transporter room simply evaporates, to be replaced by the new room to which you travel. The process occurs so quickly as to create the illusion that the room itself actually goes through the transformation.

The room in which we appeared contained half a dozen overstuffed easy chairs set around a small table. On one wall, a small viewing port about the size of a movie screen in a multiplex theater looked out upon the cosmos. Four chairs sat directly in front of it.

As soon as we entered, the three or four Verdants who were in the room took one look at Martin and hastily left. That was my first inkling that he was an authority figure. In fact, Martin had been specially selected from among the top echelon of ship's officers to personally brief me. His job was to explain to me in simple layman's terms the reasons for the recall of all the Ambassadors, the nature of the discussions that had been taking place in face-to-face conferences (including the current one involving the other humans I had met), and the issues and concerns that had prompted these extraordinary encounters.

We settled into the chairs around the table and Martin got right to the point. The Verdants had become concerned with what they were seeing in the past year or so with respect to the human condition. He explained that after the disintegration of the Soviet Union and the end of the extremely dangerous Cold War at the end of the 1980s and the beginning of the 1990s, the Verdants were pleased. They became convinced that for the first time in humankind's history, the possibility of world peace was at long last at hand.

They were so sure, in fact, that the '90s would see a transformation in the habits and attitudes of the human species that we would be ripe for induction into the Intergalactic Federation of Sovereign Planets (IFSP) within the first decade of the 21st century—the new millennium.

"It's that bedeviling diversity of the human species that has been causing us so many problems," he said. "We have so little experience with it"—he was talking specifically about the human condition—"that it appears we may have miscalculated the full ramifications. The truth is, we may have made a mistake. And I for one, at the age of 3,640 of your years, can recall only occasionally a Verdant admitting that a mistake was made. It's maddening."

His face was animated, or as much as a Verdant face can appear animated. I was perplexed.

"But isn't that impossible?" I asked. "On my first visit to the ship, you told me that Verdants have absolute intelligence. How can you make a mistake?"

Both Gina and Martin eyed me.

"You're forgetting your dreams," Gina said. "Perhaps we overloaded you with too much information. It may have been unrealistic to expect you to recall all of the details."

Ah, yes, the dreams again. As I noted earlier when describing my reunion with Gina back at the house, I had them in volumes after my return from the ship during my first visit in 1997. Because of their realism, their cohesiveness, clarity, and logical order, and the lack of chaos and symbolism that typifies most dreams, I finally became aware that they were more than mere nocturnal fantasies. Over a period of months, the Verdants had been planting information into my head.

"How can I forget?" I said. "They were so realistic."

"Well, in one of those dreams you had a conversation in which this very subject was discussed." The subject to which she referred, of course, was absolute intelligence.

After some prompting, details of that particular dream began coming back to me. In it, I had been talking with several Verdants and inquired offhandedly if they had discovered time travel or whether it is even possible to travel through time, either backward or forward.

The answer was no. And yes.

According to the information I received in this dream, the Verdants have not been able to unlock that tantalizing door, although it has not been for lack of trying—literally for millions of years. They developed several methods that in theory had promised a breakthrough, but none bore fruit. The upshot was that they have never physically traveled to other times, either past or future, to actually interact in that time framework.

"So that means it's not possible then," I said.

"What leads you to that conclusion?" one of the Verdants asked, a response I hadn't expected.

"Well, since you have achieved absolute intelligence and you haven't been able to solve the problem, then it stands to reason that it can't be done," I said.

"Absolute intelligence doesn't equate to perfection, though," I was told.

I stared at them blankly as I let the information sink in. Of course he was right. The biological brain cannot exceed the limits of its capabilities. And that's all absolute intelligence is: reaching a place where it is impossible to go any further. Perhaps the answer to time travel lies just beyond that impenetrable threshold, or at least beyond the Verdants' enormous abilities.

"We make mistakes," I was told in the dream. "Not often, and not big ones, but it does happen on occasion. We don't have all of the answers because we are not perfect and never will be."

Perhaps it will take the discovery of a new species that has the potential to become even more intelligent than the Verdants to solve the riddle of time travel. Who knows, perhaps it might even be humans who will find the key after we achieve our own level of absolute intelligence, however far into the future that may be.

Back in the here and now, Martin was reminding me about this limitation.

"There is only one perfect being. We are not gods; we are mortals. Very advanced mortals, admittedly, but mortals nevertheless. And as such we theoretically are prone to mistakes, although as I said, this would be one of those rare instances if it turned out to be true."

"What specifically is the problem?" I asked with a vague sense of uneasiness.

He explained that the various Ambassadors, all experts in their fields covering the whole arena of human endeavor, were engaged in an ongoing series of conferences with representatives of the so-called Ad Hoc Committee for Coordination of Earth Contact (AHCCEC), the specially appointed group of Verdants introduced in my first book, to thrash out the problems and arrive at solutions for ensuring that there would be no disruption of the timetable.

The issues under discussion were too numerous to mention, he told me, but he gave me a synopsis of some of the problem areas. The biggest concern, he said, was essentially this: The expected post–Cold War transformation of our global society, however gradual—in which the more decent and civilized people of the world took control of governments and institutions—was not occurring at the pace that had been anticipated.

In many respects, he said, the human condition was actually deteriorating rather than improving as it should have. Ominously, he suggested that a grand conspiracy may have been concocted by forces that oppose the contact, and that there appeared to be a deliberate campaign to stir up as much trouble as possible to discourage the Verdants from following through on their plans. The current discussions between Ambassadors and AHCCEC representatives were thus focusing on this overarching issue as well as on other existing afflictions of the human condition and the efforts being made on Earth to address them.

While Gina had already explained to me that I would have no participatory role in the conferences, I thought it would be acceptable to at least observe the proceedings. This was my chance to get permission.

"I'd like to sit in on a few of those meetings," I said.

"For what purpose?" Martin responded. He looked at Gina. "You explained the situation to him, didn't you?" Gina nodded.

I had never noticed this in any Verdant before, but Martin struck me as someone with an attitude, which in itself struck me as paradoxical because that implies an obvious display of emotion. And trying to detect an emotion in a Verdant mannerism or speech is like trying to eyeball a crystal of sugar in a shalt shaker. It could have been my imagination because, as with any such display in the Verdants, it would be extremely subtle, unrecognizable except to the trained eye. And even then it could be missed.

"Well, it could be educational," I said almost defensively. "To hear first-hand the issues they are discussing and what progress they are making might provide me with some important insights."

"You would have nothing to contribute, nor would you be likely to benefit by merely observing," Martin replied, with just the slightest sense of iciness to his tone, or so it seemed to me. "You certainly must be aware that some of the brightest minds in the universe, specifically members of our species, are engaged in scholarly discussions with some of the most intelligent people of your species.

"You're just a journalist, and a retired one at that."

I blinked vacantly, and self-consciously felt that I must have had a silly look plastered upon my face.

"I'm sorry, I don't mean to offend," he said. "It's nothing to be ashamed of. We recognize that journalists serve an important function in your society. But, please believe me when I tell you that the discussions would be far too complex for you to follow."

I caught a glimpse of Gina but she averted her eyes. He was obviously just being honest, and may not have fully realized how hurtful his words were. Still, I couldn't resist the temptation to respond, impertinence being not totally alien to my character.

"Well," I asked, fully aware I was being childish and petulant, "can you at least tell me what they might be discussing in general terms that a person of my limited intellect could grasp?"

"Sure," Martin replied without skipping a beat. "Children killing children. A global pandemic of violence against women. Corporate greed ravishing the world's resources for their own selfish ends with no regard for the disastrous ecological and environmental legacy they leave for future generations. The airwaves filled with rancor by men and women, both secular and nonsecular, consumed by hate and narrow-mindedness. Incivility of massive proportions. Skewed values and a loss of moral direction. Apathy and unconcern for the less fortunate. Rampant child abuse, the breakdown of the family, cruelty of all sorts. Unconscionable terrorists killing and maiming innocent victims."

So far, he hadn't told me anything new. All of that has been part of the fabric of our civilization for as long as I can remember, and my experience with humans doesn't go back a millennium. Certainly this couldn't come as any surprise to them, so why the sudden concern?

". . . Third-world nations that don't have the capacity to adequately feed, clothe, shelter, and provide medical care for their citizens, squandering their paltry resources on the development of nuclear weapons. Ethnic cleansing. Pedophile clerics. The resurgence of religious and ethnic hatreds and massacres. Religious zealots who rant against government but who would establish a theocracy to impose their narrow and tyrannical dogmas upon the populace.

"A sapping of the moral spirit, a malaise of the soul. Psychotic militias, deranged cults, cultural rot embraced by millions who cheer choreographed violence in public arenas and idolize smutty radio personalities. The decline of sophistication and the celebration of mediocrity. Medical clinic bombings, homophobic madness, racism, scapegoating . . ."

"Okay, okay, I get the picture," I finally said.

"The list goes on, of course," Martin said. "Your history has been a bloody one, right from the moment that your ancestors climbed down from the trees and began walking upright."

I tried to protest, reminding him that the Verdants knew about our history when they determined that we were ready for contact and began initiating procedures. I recited the progress humankind has made over the millennia, reminding him that our world is filled with good people.

"It really is," Gina offered in my support.

"You don't have to convince me, I'm aware of the data," Martin said. "But the people responsible for the corruption are still running things, and not only are they not losing momentum, they appear to be consolidating their control. We expected the masses of decent people to begin dismantling the old order, to start taking control of their destiny. But they are showing little if any indication that they are doing so.

"That," he concluded, "is the issue that's being

discussed in the meetings."

"You don't like me, do you?" I blurted out before realizing what I had said.

"Personally, I have nothing against you. I don't dislike you. I just don't like a very large segment of your species, and I don't believe that humans are ready to be accepted into the federation. That's my personal opinion, and it is a minority one at the moment. I hope that the authorities will eventually come around to my way of thinking once the conferences have concluded."

There are times when the Verdant penchant for honesty can be downright brutal.

Under the circumstances, the question of why I was there again surfaced, and I put it to Martin. After all, Gina said that he was supposed to explain to me the purpose of my presence. Of course, I liked the idea that I was aboard. It was exciting, exhilarating. But if I was to play no active role in the proceedings, I was anxious to find out just what was expected of me.

"You were invited aboard for several reasons. You have performed a valuable service for us at great personal sacrifice," Martin said. "Your invitation, in that respect, was a courtesy. You are only one of a very select few who have gone public with your story and we are aware that you have suffered as a result. We know that we have put you in an extremely stressful situation."

"He's trying to say 'thank you,'" Gina interjected.

"Don't mention it," I said, though I wasn't interested in thanks. He said I had been invited aboard for several reasons, but so far he had mentioned only one. "So, is there an agenda for me while I'm here?" I asked.

"Another reason," Martin continued without acknowledging my comment, "is that we knew Gina would get pleasure from having you aboard. She enjoys the time she spends with you."

I looked at Gina and felt a warm bond. Her features remained passive, as always, but somehow we touched on a level that involved no physical contact and for which I lack the words to describe. She was so kind, so gentle, so caring and compassionate, I thought that if I were a Verdant or if she were a human with the same characteristics, it would be easy to fall in love with her.

"My agenda?" I repeated.

"Your agenda for the time being is just to enjoy yourself," Martin said, though I had a feeling that he wasn't being completely forthright. "Gina will keep you company. Explore the ship. Have fun. Then, right before you go back you will receive a final briefing."

Since further inquiry would be fruitless, and since I'd find out soon enough, I decided not to worry.

Martin rose and left the room, leaving Gina and me alone.

"Now what?" I said.

"Let's go have some fun," she replied.

the metaphysical universe

We found ourselves back in the observation bubble, my favorite place on the ship. Coincidentally, the moon had entered the first quarter a couple of days earlier, which meant that the back half and the front half—the one facing Earth—were both partially in light and shadow. Within a few days, Earth would be seeing a full moon while the back half where the Verdant ship was positioned would be in total darkness. Even so, due to our position and our close proximity to the moon's surface, the ship was already in total darkness, as it had been during my first time aboard.

As such, hundreds of spotlights played across the massive craft, and light from thousands of portholes shone in the darkness of space. There was a beehive of activity as scores of smaller shuttlecraft entered and exited airlocks on the *Goodwill*. As I reported after my first trip aboard, the ship has a radius of about three-quarters of a mile, or a diameter of about a mile and a half. It has 16 decks or stories along the outer rim, which is about 200 feet thick at that point, and gradually rises to its highest point of 234 decks, or about 3,000 feet thick, in the center. After we seated ourselves in the chairs that looked out through the bubble and its 360-degree panorama of the velvet blackness of space, Gina activated the filtering device that screened out all artificial light and allowed only the natural light of the universe to penetrate.

I thought that even if I had the 20,000-year life span of a typical Verdant, I would never get tired of drinking in the awesome and magnificent spectacle of millions of stars and galaxies shining like brilliant diamonds against the ebony backdrop of infinity. I was unexpectedly seized with the feeling that I was in a state of grace. I had a strong desire—and felt that it was almost possible for me to do so—to reach out into the endless void and grab a handful of stardust. It has been said that there are no atheists in foxholes, and at that moment I could actually identify with those who have related tales of profound religious experiences.

I don't know if Gina—or any other Verdant for that matter—can read human minds generally or my mind specifically, or if she is just astute, but she seems to know or at least sense what I am thinking and feeling. Her next remark reinforced that suspicion.

"You're puzzled by Paul, aren't you?"

There was no doubt that Paul was still an enigma to me.

"Yes, Paul. There's something about him that I just can't pin down. He certainly knows a lot about religion, though."

"He should."

"Why is that?"

"Are you ready for this, Mr. Atheist?" I was ready for almost anything.

"He's an angel," Gina said.

I gazed at her intensely.

"You mean he's, like, a real sweetheart? A darling man? A good guy?"

"No, I mean he's an angel, literally. Specifically, he's your guardian angel," she said.

I didn't gasp, I didn't get hysterical, I didn't even blurt out a sarcastic rejoinder. I simply sat for a moment in deep thought. Then I rose from my chair, stepped down to the recessed walkway that circled the half-sphere that enclosed us, and peered down toward the surface of the moon to see if I could make out any features at all. I had done the same thing on my first visit aboard, but to no avail. It was the same this time. The ship was completely engulfed in the moon's shadow and not a shaft of sunlight was falling upon the lunar surface for as far as I could see.

"I didn't know I had one," I said quietly as I returned to my seat. "A guardian angel, I mean."

It had been less than three years since the time when I would have contemptuously snorted at the mention of such a thing, which I considered supernatural and superstitious nonsense. But I have been coming of age and my attitudes are obviously a bit different than before.

Of course, this wasn't the first unfathomable statement to me by a Verdant about spiritual matters. When I was first aboard the ship in 1997, it wasn't long after I had brought up the subject of the metaphysical nature of the universe that I found myself hopelessly bogged down in incomprehension. I simply could not fathom most of the concepts that the Verdants tried to explain to me, even though they were laboring to define them in as simple terms as they could muster.

Reporting on these things to the general public was an even bigger challenge. For example, I reported a remarkable spiritual episode of the Verdant's leading theologian in the first book, but not satisfactorily enough for many, at least according to some of the questions and comments I have received from readers. What interested me most was the complaint from readers that what I reported seemed to contradict some of their own personal spiritual beliefs and the doctrines they embraced as part of their religious training.

Some of the more zealous ones accused me of being in league with the devil himself because anyone with any brains knows that extraterrestrial creatures are fallen angels. Others were bothered by the mere mention that extraterrestrials even exist, because they believe acceptance of their particular prophet or savior is the only way that a soul can ascend into heaven. Their particular holy book doesn't mention children of God on other planets, ergo such creatures can't exist.

During our aborted discussion on this topic on my first visit aboard, the Verdants emphasized that nothing they said in this arena should be interpreted by humans as either confirming or contradicting the validity of any human religious thought, doctrine, or practice. They are extremely mindful of the importance of religion in the lives of many individuals. I thus think it would be safe to say that no human should question his or her religious beliefs or practices on the basis of what I was told.

When I raised this matter with Paul during our initial meeting in the park nine months earlier, he explained to me that any such perceived conflict is more illusory than real. I told him that I thought the concerns were serious enough to warrant some kind of explanation—even a rudimentary one—before the Verdant-Earth summit takes place. Otherwise, I said, there could be resistance to the planned contact from those who perceive a threat to their beliefs. It would be a shame if such resistance arose over a simple misunderstanding.

Paul tried his best to put my mind at ease. But much of what he said about it was so complex that I will have to leave it up to the theologians and spiritual leaders of the world to explore when the time comes for such examination.

In the meantime, some of his comments I am able to report to you, and I recall them below. After this interlude I'll return to my conversation with Gina.

"Is there a true universal religion?" I had asked.

"No," Paul replied.

I waited for him to expand on the statement. When nothing further was forthcoming, I said, "That's it? Just 'no'?"

There are thousands of belief systems throughout the universe, he said. There are also wide variations between the teachings and practices of Earth's major religions. In addition, even among the various denominations of the same religious faith, there is often a gulf of conflicting beliefs on fundamental issues.

I then asked him if the Bible or the Koran (the only two holy books that I could name because of my pitiful lack of knowledge in this arena) were the true word of God. And here he made a startling admission.

While the Verdants' knowledge about the universe and its inhabitants is second to none, he confessed that there is one area in which they can have no authoritative knowledge or insight whatsoever. The bond between God and his various peoples is a private matter, a sacred bond that cannot be known from the outside. These covenants are not subject to judgmental scrutiny by those who are not parties to them. He admitted that he might sound like a lawyer but that was as simple as he could make it.

One person to whom I related this conversation after I returned found it absolutely implausible. So more clarificiation is obviously in order.

Say the practitioners of a particular religion believe that they are required to bow to the east five times a day, excise a certain body part, or perhaps stand on their heads and meditate for an hour a day. Such activities, considered sacred practices to the adherents, may sound goofy, barbaric, or nonsensical to someone outside their religion.

However, who is to say that God does not require that of the faithful in a particular religion?

That's all the Verdants are saying. They can have no knowledge or insight into—or judgment upon—what God requires of others nor are they privy to the covenants that bind any group to their God.

According to Paul, the Verdants do know just what God

expects of them. And they assume that those who practice faiths based upon their respective teachings or holy books know what God uniquely expects of them. But, again, these are private matters between the individuals or groups and God, he told me. Therefore, no one who is not a practitioner of a particular faith is in a position, nor has the right, to judge the merits of that belief system. The only thing the Verdants know for absolute certain about the merits of religions other than their own, he said, is that God does not enter into unholy alliances.

"I'm not sure what you are saying," I had told him.

I could see he was searching for the right words—most likely the simplest words, such as the ones that an adult would cast about for when talking to a child. Simply put, he explained, that means God does not impose consequences upon others who do not share a particular faith. In other words, if I was interpreting him correctly, he was saying that people should apply their beliefs strictly to themselves. When I asked for confirmation of my interpretation, he said that I was "in the ballpark."

I guess he thought that close wasn't good enough, because he made another stab at trying to get me to understand by saying that no creature—extraterrestrial as well as terrestrial, I suppose he meant—should expect other equally moral creatures to suffer penalties or consequences simply because they do not agree with the other's doctrines.

Since I wasn't taking notes, I can't quote him perfectly, but he was very emphatic when he said something to the effect that "Your covenant with God is your own business that applies only to you. Other creatures' relationship with God is their own personal affair that does not concern others who embrace different beliefs."

I also learned from Paul that Earth is one of the very few planets so far discovered that is so advanced technologically yet has such a multiplicity of religions, owing to the fact that our species' cultural diversity is unprecedented in the universe (insofar as they have yet discovered). Individual members of all species that belong to the intergalactic federation—at the least—are so homogenous, so alike in thinking, temperament, intelligence, and emotional makeup with all others in their group that there is but a single theology that every individual is comfortable with on each of the vast majority of planets. In other words, each species has its own worldwide belief system, set of values, and codes of conduct, as well as its own unique conventions for practicing that religion, its particular covenant with God. The Verdants themselves also have their own religion.

I'm afraid it isn't clear to me if this monotheism also extends to other less-advanced civilizations—ones that may still be in a tribal stage—that are not yet members of the federation. It makes sense, though, that societies still in the early stages of development would be divided into tribes, clans, kingdoms, nations—whatever term fits. As such, because of this separation, it seems logical that that there would be a variety of cultures, languages, and religions.

Paul had told me that he didn't want to get involved in debating the merits of any of the various human religious teachings, but one of the more intriguing bits of information I gleaned from him is that a great spiritual adventure—call it an awakening—awaits humankind when it finally becomes a member of the IFSP. He didn't elaborate.

Apparently, there are certain things that the Verdants

know for fact, either because they discovered them independently or because they were revealed to them by God. The Supreme Theologian—the spiritual leader within the intergalactic federation—has a special relationship with God in which they communicate regularly. Paul explained that he didn't mean simply a mortal supplicant praying to the Almighty and hoping his prayers would be answered. He meant that actual two-way conversations take place and that these can be scientifically and factually documented. (Incidentally, since this position is rotated among the member species of the IFSP, there will come a time when a human being presumably will hold this office.)

This was a startling concept. As an old cynic, I have never had much faith in organized religion, and it is not uncommon for my wife to hear me snort while reading the daily paper and coming across a headline proclaiming that some spiritual leader was "Praying for World Peace."

"When have humans ever had world peace?" I would ask no one in particular, especially since my wife pays no attention to my ranting about the news. "Never!" I would answer. So that means that God isn't listening or the leaders of major religions have no influence upon him. And yet now I was being told that someday a human Supreme Theologian might actually have a one-on-one discourse with God himself!

I asked Paul another question.

"What is the soul?"

I wish I could quote him exactly, but he spoke so eloquently and so wisely that I'll have to settle for paraphrasing his comments and hope that I understood correctly.

Basically he replied that it's a gift from God that sets

humans—and other intelligent creatures on other planets—apart from the lower animals. The soul, he continued, is the link between intelligent beings and God and takes the form of spirit. It is a higher level of life, if you will, a spiritual life that resides within intelligent creatures even while they conduct their mortal lives. The two lives exist side by side while the individual resides on the physical plane.

All sentient beings with souls are equal partners in the universal family, he further explained. However, contrary to whatever thoughts I did have on the subject, the soul itself is universal and does not differ from one species to the next even though individual ones may temporarily reside in creatures of different physical bodies.

That is—if I was grasping the full import of his words—a mortal creature of higher intelligence may have six legs and two heads; it may be anthropoid in form, such as the human; it may give birth to live young or lay eggs; it may have fangs or a beak; but the soul in each is identical. Consequently, despite their mortal differences, all individuals in every species are like brothers and sisters under God, the ultimate parent.

It is hardly a surprise, then, to learn that there is a universal love between the species who have progressed to the status of star travelers, since they are all of the same spiritual family. As such, Paul said, there is no place in the universal family for the odious character trait of hatred of other races or species, which is actually a form of self-loathing.

It was an inspiring pronouncement, one that certainly disputes some current theories of extraterrestrial contact suggesting that they are malevolent beings intent on harming us. Again, I am only reporting my own experience and what I was told.

The fact that all 27,000 member-species practice their own unique religions also seemed to confirm his statement that there is no one true universal religion. Paul said that the individual differences are no more significant than the mode of dress between the disparate species—or even between the various national and cultural groups of humans on Earth. The styles may differ widely, from the Western business suit to the Japanese kimono to the flowing robes of Arab desert dwellers, but they are all clothing and they all fill functional and aesthetic purposes. As such, the Supreme Theologian could serve that office faithfully no matter what religion he practiced. In the same vein, the secretary-general of the United Nations could be an effective leader no matter if he wore a suit or a robe, or if she wore a dress and high heels or a sari and sandals.

I was again tempted to ask Paul what human religion was the most legitimate vis-a-vis the IFSP ones, but of course he had already indicated that he would not presume to make any such comparison or judgment. So I asked him about the Verdant religion.

They have their ceremonies and rituals as do most other religions, he replied, but they are just that—reflections of their own cultural preferences. He emphasized that I should keep in mind that there is no right or wrong way to praise God, and that it's not the style of worship but the manner in which individuals conduct their lives that determines their piety.

Apparently, unlike many believers (including some of those on Earth), the Verdants do not regularly attend services. Their houses of worship serve primarily as teaching centers, although there is one important ceremony that is conducted there that all Verdants go through when they reach "adolescence": the time when a young person acknowledges God and promises to lead a moral life.

"No regular prayer services?" I asked Paul.

He replied that prayer is an integral part of many religions, a ritual that gives comfort to those who participate in such ceremonies. The supplicants also take the opportunity at those times to reaffirm their love of God and their vows to live moral lives. It struck me at the time that perhaps the American custom of reciting the Pledge of Allegiance offers similar (patriotic) comfort to participants.

Verdants have no such emotional needs, though, he explained. Once the young adults pledge to abide by God's laws, they consider it a lifelong covenant that does not require periodic renewal.

"It's not unlike your own marriage vows," Paul said. "You consider them binding for a lifetime or until such time as you choose to sever them."

That made sense to me; we married people don't usually see any need to go through the marriage ceremony on a daily, weekly, or monthly basis because we've already made that lifelong commitment.

"How did the Verdants prove the existence of the soul?" I asked.

I finally thought I had stumped him, and all he gave was an assurance that they knew and that it was somehow linked to the Verdant life span. That is, the research that allowed them to keep extending their lives until it reached the point where it is today—approximately 20,000 Earth years—also opened doors that led to discovery of the existence of the soul.

His revelations just kept bowling me over. I had gone up to the ship an atheist and come back as something else, and after talking with Paul that day my spiritual identity was vaguer still. I still consider myself a humanist of sorts, but not necessarily a secular humanist anymore. Is there such a thing as a nonsecular or spiritual humanist? Is that an oxymoron? I just don't know. I'm not reluctant to admit that I'm still very confused these days.

And now here I was with Gina, who was telling me that Paul is an angel—my angel. It had been nearly two years earlier, in April 1998, when I actually did see an apparition at a talk given by renowned author Dr. Doreen Virtue, a respected researcher on the subject of angels. (See the Reporter's Notebook in Part 2.) However, what I saw then was an obvious apparition, and Paul did not take that form. He definitely was flesh and blood as far as I could tell.

"Most people go through their whole lives and are never aware of them," Gina said.

"So, tell me more about Paul. How come I can see him? I thought angels were supposed to be invisible, with wings and stuff."

"Invisible, yes. Wings, no. Paul's current form is only temporary. It's an expediency to complete his assignment, to allow you to see him in the flesh, so to speak. To let you know that he is there."

According to Gina, Paul has been looking after me, especially for the last several years. Most of the time his presence isn't detectable, but he does take on mortal form on occasion when circumstances warrant it. The first time I met him, he chose the human configuration because we met in a public park and others might have considered it a bit eccentric to see me engaged in animated conversation with myself. And he currently was in a human body so that he could interact with the Ambassadors while also connecting with me. Gina said that I was the only human aboard who now knew that Paul was not one of us. The Verdants, of course, were aware of it.

"Why has he been keeping an eye on me?" I asked.

She told me that the nature of my assignment on the Verdants' behalf placed me in a somewhat vulnerable position, although as a matter of routine the Verdants instituted security precautions to ensure that it didn't become perilous. This was news to me, although I had actually become more security conscious after the unannounced visit to my home by X and the "outed" Ambassador who had advised me to be vigilant.

But if Paul was looking after me, why was it necessary for X to offer such advice? Certainly, as a key player at the time, he must have known that security precautions had been instituted for my benefit. Was it possible that even a guardian angel could not guarantee absolute safety 24 hours a day? And how much did X know about the details of these security measures? After all, Gina had just finished telling me that I was the only human aboard who was aware of Paul's real identity. Did that mean that no Ambassador knew I had a guardian angel, or just the ones currently on the ship? I asked Gina for an explanation.

She said that X knew only that I was being protected; he was not aware of the details. Without that knowledge, his advice about being vigilant was sound on the reasonable assumption that one can never be too careful under the circumstances.

"You have never been in any real danger; Paul has seen to that. That's his job. But you do remember the threatening letters and e-mail messages?" she asked. "Remember the time you almost got run down by a truck when you were jogging? Then there were the ominous and anonymous phone calls; the requests from strangers who wanted to set up personal meetings with you; and the time you stumbled on the escalator at the mall and thought you were going to take a disastrous fall."

I did receive some strange mail, including several threatening letters, but I never paid too much attention to them because I figured the writers were just harmless cranks. However, according to Gina, Paul visited the writers to check them out and to ensure that they were just that—harmless. And in his own creative way, he made sure that the writers did not repeat their offenses.

One particular piece of mail stuck out in my mind as I was thinking about what Gina was saying. It was a plain off-white envelope addressed to me at my home that contained an unsigned letter. The envelope, bearing a Washington, D.C., postmark dated October 9, 1998, had no return address. This is what the letter said.

TRUST NO ONE!

By the time you receive this, you will no doubt have heard the news about Art Bell. He has been silenced.
You have already been contacted by the UFO lawyer.
Be advised that you have adversaries, to put it mildly, and

enemies, to put it in the strongest terms. Some of these interests, international in scope, are working in concert. Some are natural rivals, openly hostile to one another, operating under conflicting agendas but with a common goal.

You represent forces that are a threat to their purposes. They want you silenced also. They routinely use the tools of threats and intimidation. If necessary, they will attempt to discredit you.

Certain of your adversaries, enemies, have the ability to access every record and file ever compiled on you. Bear in mind that records and files can be doctored and falsified.

Remember, trust no one. That is your best protection.

Of course, Art Bell—a popular late-night radio talk-show host who routinely deals with offbeat topics, including metaphysical concepts, extraterrestrial intelligence, and related subjects—returned to the air shortly afterward, although he later resigned in early 2000, and then returned once again to the air. I don't know what to make of the statement regarding his having been silenced. Nevertheless, I took that letter to heart. I don't know who sent it, but it felt like it was from someone who is informed, who is staying current with developments in the UFO/alien-abduction field. Could it have been from an Ambassador? The reader's guess is as good as mine.

"Trust no one!" What cynical advice. But considering the number of people in the field with different agendas, the variety of theories and belief systems, the diverse personality types, the sparring and jarring and jockeying for position, the feuding and fussing between the various personalities, I think it's good advice.

I thought about another correspondence, an e-mail, that arrived on March 26, 1998. It was sent to my publisher and forwarded to me and contained an ominous statement that I didn't pay much attention to at the time.

The writer asked me if I would be willing to contact a person associated with CSETI (Center for the Study of Extraterrestrial Intelligence) to possibly join a group of scientists, former astronauts, military personnel, and others pushing for the establishment of congressional hearings on the UFO phenomenon. My testimony was being solicited in the event those hearings ever materialized. That letter read in part:

> *Individuals can be ridiculed where their message is smothered. Or . . . I think of former Congressman Steven Schiff, who died of skin cancer. He was investigating the Roswell crash a while back. I wouldn't be surprised if some agency just wanted to shut him up. A large group testifying nationwide with "everyone" listening and watching will help protect you from any threats that can come up all of a sudden.*
>
> *Your phone, your personal hygiene products can be tampered with, and your home can be burned down to quiet you. Even* [the person he wanted me to contact] *may warn you that the possibility of your testifying could be a threat to some sinister group or agency.*

I determined then that I would be more diligent in watching my back, but I was not going to be deterred either.

A number of people made requests to meet privately with me, although I rarely granted such solicitations. Even so, Paul apparently checked them out as well and did determine that one person among the dozen or so who had made such requests was unbalanced. According to Gina, he saw to it that the person would not be a threat to me. I didn't want to know the details, though I don't suppose guardian angels actually go around roughing up people and telling them to back off. But who knows? Just one more eye-opening revelation.

The truck incident occurred a couple of weeks before Christmas in 1998, I believe. I was on my daily jog around my housing development, running on the sidewalk, when I crossed a driveway that leads into a gated community encompassed by my neighborhood. The driveway is one of four that access the community, and is about 40 or 50 feet wide where it crosses the sidewalk. It was dark at the time, sometime close to six o'clock.

Normally I would have yielded to the vehicle as it exited the gate, but I was nearly halfway across the driveway when the truck came roaring out of the gate with no apparent intention of stopping. I was caught squarely in its headlights, and just when I thought I was going to be hit the truck jerked to a stop only inches away.

I kept running, figuring that the driver was simply not paying attention. To my stunned surprise, he let loose a string of obscenities as I continued down the sidewalk, as though he were disappointed that he had missed me and was venting his frustration. What a moron, I had thought at the time.

According to Gina, Paul had actually braked the truck. As it turned out, the driver did not even live in the area, she said. Paul determined later that the driver was from Las Vegas and had a criminal record. Was he deliberately trying to hurt me? Gina said they hadn't yet made that conclusion, but they were suspicious. Still, they don't believe that it was an organized attempt on my life because the circumstances were too haphazard.

I never gave much thought to the escalator incident, assuming that I had just been clumsy. Gina said that I had been pushed, and again the intended result was merely to harm me rather than kill me. Unknown to me at the time, Paul had yanked my right hand onto the handrail and pulled me backward to allow me to regain my balance.

This was really getting bizarre. I could understand if the perpetrators were simply mentally unbalanced, part of the vast army of loners, losers, and lunatics who periodically embark upon psychotic missions that make sense only in their troubled minds. That happens all the time. The media have given extensive coverage to politicians, TV and movie stars, sports figures, and other high-profile personalities who have fallen victim to stalkers and assassins over the years.

But let's assume I had been deliberately targeted for some particularly logical reason. What could be the motivation?

In a word—intimidation, Gina explained. Any suspicious harm that came to me would send a very powerful message to other Deputy Envoys and Ambassadors who have not yet revealed themselves. They might become too fearful to follow through on their assignments, which could disrupt the whole process. Or at least that is the thinking by the forces of opposition, she said. That would simply be but one step in their total strategy because they are operating on many fronts.

"The whole purpose is to sabotage the contact."

"Are they really that well organized?" I asked.

"I'm afraid so. And their network is worldwide. A lot is at stake on both sides."

"So, I ask again, as I have asked others on several occasions: Am I in danger?"

"You'll be fine. No one is going to get past Paul."

That was certainly comforting.

"You must be hungry," she said. "Let's go get you some sustenance."

She deactivated the filter and the giant ship flared into view again outside the bubble, lit up by the massive floodlights that played over it, the seemingly thousand glowing portholes. Without the corruption of artificial lights, the inside of the half-sphere where we had been sitting was quite dark, illuminated only by the billions of stars and galaxies to a level of perhaps one-quarter as bright as a moonlit night on Earth. But with the filter deactivated, the artificial lights emanating from the ship itself lightened the room considerably, allowing us to see each other clearly and navigate without missteps.

As we stepped down from the raised viewing platform that held the seats, Gina continued on down to the walkway that circled the room rather than heading for the door.

"You'll probably want to see this," she said.

She raised her arm at a 70-degree angle and pointed a delicately thin index finger.

"See that really bright object about 10 o'clock high?"

I craned my neck to see where she was looking. The object was impossible to miss because of its brilliance. It was the brightest thing in the "sky" and stood out in dazzling domination among the millions of other points of light.

It was, in fact, an amazing spectacle.

"What is it?" I asked.

"It's a meteoroid, just an errant hunk of rock, or more likely iron," Gina said. "It's coming this way."

"But why is it glowing? There's no atmosphere, so it can't be burning up. It should really be invisible."

"It's being burned up by an atomizer, an energy beam." She turned her finger toward the ship and said that the beam was emanating from a special port deep within the ship's superstructure. The closest that Gina could come to describing it was to compare it to what we humans know as high-powered lasers, a still-crude comparison. And unlike a laser, the beam itself was invisible.

"What's going to happen? How big is that thing, anyway? Is it going to come close to us, or hit the moon, or what?" It was a thrilling moment and a thousand questions raced through my mind.

"It's about a meter in diameter—a yard in your measurement system—but we can't let it hit the moon even at that size. It would cause an awfully big explosion."

The object seemed to be growing in size, and then it blinked out.

"They got it," Gina said.

"How far away was it?" I asked.

"Probably about 20 miles at its last moment. There was plenty of time to spare. It would have taken another 3 or 4 seconds to get here."

Another drifting booby trap eliminated. It's a routine procedure that goes on all the time, I was told.

Suddenly, a paralyzing chill swept through my body. For the first time during either of my visits aboard, I felt a deep, cold fear. Not anxiety, not apprehension, not mere alarm. This was sheer, numbing dread that reached inside my chest and clutched my heart in an icy grip.

I thought I had caught them in a lie! And if they had lied to me about this, what else had they lied to me about?

"That could be used as a weapon of mass destruction!" I blurted out. "You have weapons aboard this ship!"

Curse those passive faces. It was so difficult to read anything on them. What was I seeing, if anything? A touch of impatience, perhaps?

"You really are a skeptic," she said. "You take a lot of convincing. Just when we think we've reached you, developed a mutual bond of trust and respect, you continue to raise challenges.

"However, listen to me carefully now. There are no weapons in space. *They aren't allowed.*" She put great emphasis on the words.

And then the strangest thing happened. A little sound escaped from her mouth and I could read just the faintest hint of frustration on her face. An equivalent human reaction would be an animated expression of total exasperation with an accompanying "aaaarrrrrrggggggghhhhhh." It was the most emotion I had ever witnessed in any of these creatures.

"The atomizer is totally harmless to living organisms, both animal and vegetable," she said after a pause. "You could stand directly in front of it and it wouldn't so much as singe an eyelash. It is effective only against inanimate objects. It is a tool."

The words were comforting and my initial reaction of horror began abating, but I pointed out that a spaceship is an inanimate object that could be filled with living organisms. Even if the ray weren't harmful against living organisms, blasting a spaceship out of existence wouldn't be very healthy for the people inside. She further explained that the energy ray penetrates to the very core of every atom in the targeted object. If a single living cell is detected, the beam passes harmlessly through.

"Let's say that the meteoroid contained a living bacterium inside its core," she said, "a simple one-celled animal. We would know immediately that there was life aboard when the rock or hunk of iron failed to atomize when the beam struck it."

I believed her. "What would you do then?"

"If there was time, send a shuttlecraft out to snare it and bring it back to the laboratory for study," she replied. "Otherwise we would do nothing except take evasive action if we were about to be hit by it. If it was going to miss the moon, then the shuttle craft would chase it down and capture it."

Once analyzed, the rock would be crushed into harmless dust and sprinkled back into space. Larger objects, let's say the size of a modern aircraft carrier or larger, would be studied on site and then eventually catapulted toward the nearest star, where they would be consumed. And the solar system would be just a little bit safer from wandering marauders.

Now I felt a lot better. We returned to my quarters and Gina sat with me as I ate. I figured it was by now about 2 p.m. Sunday afternoon back in California.

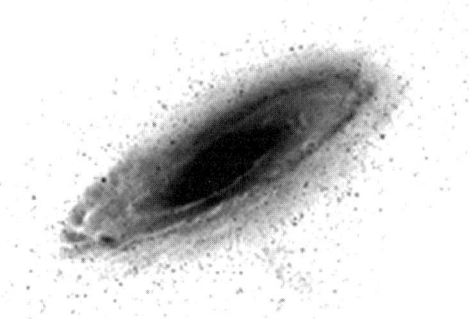

revelations

It had been almost two years since I last spoke with X, but my curiosity about the strange ending of our meeting at my house had not diminished.

I asked Gina if she had any knowledge about him that she could share with me as I chowed down on meatless T-bone steak, garlic toast, carrot and raisin salad, baked potato with sour cream and butter, and lemonade. (Just where they came up with such menus I couldn't fathom.) I mentioned the circumstances and explained to her that X and I had been getting along fine until the final moments when I apparently said something that caused him to become furious.

"Don't take it personally," Gina said. "He's angry about a lot of things and sometimes takes it out on others. He's an angry person."

I asked if X had been brought back up for his briefing conference yet and was puzzled to learn that not only had he not been up but that he would not be coming up. Gina seemed to choose her words very carefully. She was always cooperative in answering my questions in a general way, but at some points in our conversation she was reluctant to go into details. This was one of those times. Since I wasn't included in the inner circle of those participating in the meetings, I understood her caution. Those people, after all, were carrying out the bulk of the heavy responsibilities while I wasn't much more than a messenger.

"Can you at least tell me what happened?" I asked. "If X isn't going to participate in the conferences, that might imply that he's no longer playing a key role in the program."

X had been given the responsibility for planning and eventually overseeing the worldwide dissemination of the story once the decision was made to break the news of the impending summit conference between the human and Verdant species. It would not be an exclusive *L.A. Times* story, even though X held an important position there. The plan called for all information and photos to be shared with every major news-gathering organization in the world. It would be the job of the *Times* Ambassador to administer and oversee that phase of the operation.

His plan had to indicate the tactics, strategy and logistics that would be employed to ensure that the world's news organizations had access to every shred of information that became available. In effect, a totally new worldwide communications network, with the *Times* as the nerve center, would have to be established.

"It would be logical to infer that," Gina said in response to my speculation. "As for what happened, all I can say is that he is no longer an Ambassador and therefore not involved in the process. I'm sure you're aware of the shake-up that has been going on at that newspaper."

The *Times* had in fact been caught recently in a conflict of interest involving some of the people in the highest levels of management, which caused a minor rebellion among the reporters and lower-level editors. Not only was I kept apprised of the situation by one of my contacts at the plant as it was developing, but the paper also ran a series of stories on the scandal in an attempt at damage control. Executives had begun abandoning the paper several years preceding the current brouhaha because of conflicts with the new management team, and the exodus was continuing.

[On March 13, 2000, two months after my conversation with Gina, the *Times* announced that it would be acquired by the Tribune Company of Chicago, thereby ending more than 100 years of local ownership. Naturally, that meant that the CEO would be out of a job. While both the publisher and the editor indicated that they had no intention of resigning, the *Times* reported the following month that both would be replaced by *Tribune* people.]

I didn't know at the time of my talk with Gina if X was still employed there, but I intended to place a phone call when I returned home to satisfy my curiosity. One thing was certain—he was no longer in charge of the press operations. I have no idea what effect that will have on the timetable or whether he has been replaced by another Ambassador.

In fact, the sale of the *Times* at this particular juncture raises a series of phenomenal questions and poses serious doubts about whether the timing was mere coincidence.

That is, was X's role discovered? Did some powerful force determine that the way to deal with a situation that threatened its influence was to neutralize it? Did X himself stumble upon information that caused him to have a change of mind? Was he outed? Threatened? Is there a group opposed to the contact that is so powerful that it can reach into the highest corporate and media echelons to influence decisions?

I am not a conspiracy theorist, and I don't believe that I am paranoid, but the list of questions is endless.

I finished my lunch, and right on cue a Verdant entered and removed the food cart.

We spent the next several hours strolling through the ship. Actually, we did more than just stroll. We teletransported—at least that's what I call it. We rode what I presumed were elevators to various decks. At one point, we took a tram and traveled through a labyrinth of what appeared to be a series of connected laboratories, where I witnessed hundreds of Verdants engaged in a variety of esoteric and mystifying procedures, some of them using instruments and machines of such an obscure and shadowy nature that they were absolutely meaningless to me.

The tram, incidentally, was like nothing I had ever ridden on. It appeared to follow a predetermined path, but there were no rails. In fact, it even lacked wheels. It was a simple open-cabin affair, although quite sleek and elegant, that moved along its course suspended a fraction of an inch above the floor. Each car could accommodate two bodies sitting side by side, something akin to a roller coaster car. The cars were not attached to one another and moved independently and silently. No steering was necessary.

To board one of the cars, the traveler simply stood at a designated spot and the next empty car passing by would stop to allow embarkation. A single button on a console was pushed to bring the car to a stop to allow the passenger to disembark. I don't know how many cars were in operation, but they traversed the route in a constant circular stream, stopping only to take on or let off passengers.

Among the places that Gina and I visited was the enclave where the "energy beams" are generated, a term that meant virtually nothing to me. If anything, the closest thing I could compare it to would be an astronomical observatory, and even that is a crude example. I suspect that we wound up there because Gina was still attempting to reassure me, although it wasn't necessary. In essence, her actions were saying, "See, everything is open to you. We have no secret weapons."

But there was one particular subject that I wanted to bring up with her during this period of time together.

Earlier in the week, I had received an e-mail message from a retired Los Angeles Police Department detective who was curious as to whether the Verdants had the ability to become invisible. I told him that I had no knowledge one way or the other and so couldn't answer his question, which I nonetheless found captivating. I reasoned that if it were at all possible for mortal beings to become invisible, then it's also possible that a very technologically advanced species that had attained absolute intelligence might very well have discovered the key to unlock that door.

When I asked Gina about it, she was quite forthright and said that attaining invisibility is a fairly simple procedure that even humans would probably be capable of achieving before the end of the 21st century.

"It really doesn't have many practical applications, though. Basically, it's not much more than a toy. Our children actually play several games that involve invisibility," she said.

Was she serious? I could think of dozens of applications for invisibility, but then it occurred to me that I was thinking in culture-locked terms. If I know anything about human nature, I think the first place that the average male would head if he could become invisible would be the women's locker room at the local college. On a less frivolous note, invisibility would be a great tool for international espionage, spying on suspected wayward spouses, cleaning out bank vaults, harassing people with whom we have grudges, and so on.

But again, my thinking was restricted by my own cultural experiences. Henry Ford once said that thinking is the most difficult work of all. I can go him one better: Thinking beyond the limitations of the totality of one's experience, outside the bounds of cultural influence, is even harder. My concepts of how invisibility could be put to use were so shallow as to be embarrassing. None of the situations that I could envision had even the remotest application to the Verdant way of life as I understand it.

Peeping? Spying? Stealing? Harassing foes? Unfortunately, such petty and contemptible behaviors are easily recognizable as characteristically human. They certainly are totally foreign when considered in a Verdant context. Besides, Gina told me, there are so many other ways of detecting a body's presence that invisibility would provide no cover whatsoever. Body heat, sound, movement, slight fluctuations in air currents in a room as the result of normal respiration, imperceptible odors that all organisms emit, the pressure of a body against the floor, even brain waves from the invisible subject, were just some of the examples that Gina cited as telltale signs that can be picked up by sensors.

Nevertheless, I wouldn't mind having such a toy. There are a couple of people to whom I'd like to deliver a swift kick in the pants without being detected. That could be fun.

I figured it was about 8 p.m. or thereabouts on Sunday at home when Gina suggested that I might be ready for my next meal. I was a bit hungry and, I must admit, a quick visit to the restroom would be appreciated. There was no shortage of water whenever I became thirsty during my periods outside of my sleeping quarters—all I had to do was mention it and a Verdant would be there at my side with a container of the fresh, clean, cool liquid. I drank straight from the container, which was not that far different than a pint-size bottle of drinking water that one can find in any supermarket. But the container was neither plastic nor glass. It was transparent, but I would not even hazard a guess at its composition.

While I had no trouble requesting water, I could not bring myself to ask about a restroom. First, it would have been slightly embarrassing, and second, I wasn't sure that there were facilities outside of the guest rooms that accommodated humans. I was too nervous about using one of the Verdant facilities—I had no idea what form such equipment would take or whether it would be adaptable to human needs.

So the first thing I did when we got back to my quarters was to excuse myself. When I emerged, there was no food cart to greet me, which was a first. It turned out that Gina had made other arrangements. We joined a small group of other Verdants in a little room that took us just a couple of minutes to get to via a short walk, a quick soundless rail ride, and one final walk of a couple of hundred feet.

"I thought you might enjoy some other company," she said as we approached the room. "Besides, the ones we are going to meet are anxious to talk with you. They're very curious, naturally, since they are Verdants."

The other humans whom I had met would not be joining us; in fact, they were themselves at that moment being fed as a group in a makeshift dining area. I thought it was a bit peculiar that I had been excluded from that affair since it was just dinner and not a business meeting, but then maybe business was being discussed informally. I was glad that Gina had taken it upon herself to see that I didn't spend the rest of the evening alone in my quarters.

There were six other Verdants in the room with Gina and me, and we spent several hours chatting amiably on a number of topics. As usual, none of the Verdants ate as I busied myself with my plate of food. The Verdants theselves eat but one meal in a 36-hour cycle, I was told, and I never saw them partake of any food. Even so, I was never self-conscious and my appetite was not diminished by the fact that I alone was eating. Each one displayed an impressive store of knowledge about the human species, and they asked some provocative and penetrating questions.

For example, one of my hosts displayed what I interpreted as perplexed curiosity when she asked me about the "peculiar and quaint" custom in which professionals such as surgeons, teachers, police officers, etc., received less remuneration than others who pretend to be professionals.

The question stumped me. I asked her to explain, and when she did I was momentarily left speechless.

She was talking about actors!

As the Verdants saw it, why would a brain surgeon, highly skilled, better educated, and likely more intelligent, be paid less for performing a life-saving procedure than someone who pretended to be doing identical work?

Why indeed? I found the question delightful and intriguing. I couldn't answer it, but I reveled in the intellectual stimulation.

There were other whimsical moments when I felt as though I were a specimen under a microscope being studied by a group of postgraduate students. But they were simply exhibiting an intense curiosity and I was enjoying the exchange, perhaps even flattered by the attention. And they were altogether gracious.

During the course of our friendly give-and-take, I brought up the subject of reincarnation. It was something I never believed in and never really gave much thought to, but I had received a number of inquiries from readers who were keenly interested in the subject. Under ordinary circumstances, I would have been completely astounded by the response I got. (A Verdant wearing the name tag "Clarence" did most of the talking.) But I was on a spaceship, surrounded by aliens, my second time aboard, and my life had taken so many bizarre twists and turns in the last couple of years that I could more easily accept revelations that previously might have knocked me for a loop.

Although they have no personal experience with reincarnation, the Verdants do have reason to believe that there may be times when some individuals among certain species undergo that metamorphic phenomenon.

"It hasn't been proven," Clarence said, "but there is solid evidence that points to the possibility. However, it has no application to the Verdant experience. If it did, we undoubtedly would have confirmed it by now. The human is one of just a few species that we have come across in which some individuals might experience such a transformation."

He explained that the Verdants had created a form of hypnotic deep-mind probe that occasionally produces puzzling results. Some subjects who have undergone testing appear to have retrieved memories that can't be explained by their current existence. In fact, Verdant scientific teams have dissected and analyzed these mysterious and inexplicable memories and have been able to link them, in a very few instances, to the lives of previously deceased individuals.

That's a paraphrase of the way I understood what he was saying. But when I wrinkled my brow and scratched my head in seeming incomprehension, "Bernice" tried to simplify it for me.

"It means that the memories aren't consistent with the life of the subject being tested. So we take those memories and try to find corresponding events with previous lives. In a few very rare cases, we have been able to find a relationship between the memories and the lives of some deceased individuals. For instance, let's say the subject remembers being a particular historical figure. We then look through the records and try to find some parallels with the memories."

Of course, if the subject really had been reincarnated, there would be no way of making such comparisons if he or she had not left a public record of his/her existence. A totally anonymous person in a previous life would leave no such record, and thus no comparison could be made.

"So, that's why you've rarely been able to make connections?" I asked.

"Correct," Bernice said.

Which means that there could be many more examples of possible reincarnations but the Verdants can't reconcile the memories. Even though I didn't believe in reincarnation, I am no different than most other humans who periodically have flashes of disconnected memory that seem to come out of nowhere and exist independently from our own experiences. Typically we just shrug them off, but maybe there really is something more to them.

It seemed to me that a biographer or a history buff who was intimately familiar with the details of a historical figure's life could easily fool the probe by providing information in the guise of fake memories that coincided with events in the life of the deceased person. Apparently that wouldn't work, though, because the probe can isolate real memories from learned material.

"Anyway, we simply have suspicions," Clarence said. "We are not yet convinced one way or the other. Even if reincarnation is not a reality, we are extremely interested in discovering the source of these enigmatic memories. We'll find the answer someday."

It was all so utterly fascinating that I started to feel fortunate to have missed the private dinner party with the other humans on board; it would probably have been no different than the awkward reception of the previous night.

"Do you use drugs?" I asked, and the moment the words were out of my mouth I realized that I had misspoken. Again. Naturally, all eyes turned to me, and I started laughing at my own bumbling. "No, I mean, when you do the hypnosis, the mind-probe thing, do you use drugs in the test?"

Maybe it was the late night, the long day, the sheer magnitude of it all, but I just couldn't stop giggling. Fortunately, I knew that the Verdants have a sense of humor, because earlier in our conversation a Verdant named Joseph asked me if I knew anything about the dynamics of stars, specifically the conversion of hydrogen into helium by the tremendous pressure at the star's core, which leads to a thermonuclear reaction. Or something like that. Whatever he said, it was news to me.

"Are you kidding? I don't even know how my sunscreen works," I said.

Seven dispassionate faces gazed at me and I noticed that the index finger of Joseph's right hand, which was resting on the arm of his chair, began a rapid, rhythmic tapping. Immediately, all of the others began to mimic the motion with their own fingers. Then, in another breakthrough in reading their emotions, I recognized on each face an ever-so-slight change in expression in the musculature around the mouth and eyes that I had noticed earlier on Gus when I thought that he was grinning at me.

They were all laughing uproariously! The tapping finger was apparently equivalent to a human slapping his thigh in a belly-busting guffaw.

I grinned in return, and the episode lasted for a good 15 seconds as the ETs looked from one to the other as humans would in sharing a wonderful joke with each other. Finally, things settled down, although a human who was meeting these creatures for the first time probably would not have noticed the distraction.

Anyway, as to my query about drugs, none are used in the process of memory retrieval. From what I could understand, the subject merely lies on whatever surface is provided, relaxes, and an electronic gizmo does the actual probing. The subject doesn't even have to communicate what is occurring in his or her mind. The probe transcends the conscious mind, bypasses all memories that are related to current existence, and seeks out and electronically records memory bank anomalies, those inexplicable little aberrations that simply shouldn't be there. In the vast majority of cases, nothing unusual turns up. The rare instance occurs in a tiny minority of individuals within an even smaller number of species.

"And no explanation for it?" I asked.

"None. Interestingly, though, the memories occur only in those few species in which the culture exhibits some belief in reincarnation, however minimal. We have never found these mystical memories in any individual of any species whose culture is devoid of such beliefs. We're not sure yet what to make of that," Clarence said.

Only in the last couple of years had I become aware of the vast numbers of people who believe in reincarnation, that life is lived over and over again until the person finally gets it right. For Hindus and some Buddhists, the concept is actually at the center of their spiritual practice. I was curious to see if I could discover some insights about it, to learn if there really was a reasonable or rational basis for what I considered a rather bizarre idea.

One firm believer with whom I had a conversation some months earlier told me that she believes that the world keeps getting better and the human condition continues to evolve to higher and higher moral and ethical planes precisely because of reincarnation. As time passes, she explained, larger and larger segments of the population move into the final stages of these series of lives. As a consequence, with more and more people living more decent lives, the world itself becomes a better place. Eventually, she said, everyone on Earth will be in that final stage and the world itself will be transformed—Utopia will have been achieved. I wondered if that theory could explain the 80-20 percent concept held by the Verdants.

"So, how do you pick your subjects?" I asked as calmly as I could, eager to have my own mind probed for evidence of other lives.

"Volunteers," Bernice responded.

"I would be willing if you are interested," I said hopefully.

"How about first thing tomorrow after your sleep period?" Clarence said.

"Great," I exclaimed, relieved at the ease of their agreement and excited at the prospect of what I might find out.

It was finally time to say goodnight, and so Gina escorted me to my room. After she left, I brushed my teeth, took a leisurely shower, and slipped into fresh garments. I lay on the bed, thought momentarily of turning on the TV. As I reported after my first visit to the ship, the room itself seemed to be right out of a Holiday Inn—albeit a very modern one—and contained a big-screen color television set. Previously, I had surfed through about 500 channels, finding all of the major networks and premium channels—the whole range of what I could find on my own TV at home—and much, much more. But I was in no mood to watch anything this time so I tossed the remote control aside and decided to just go to sleep. As usual, the lights dimmed to a comfortable sleeping level but with enough illumination to make out objects in the room.

But sleep never came. I kept tossing and turning, anticipating the probe but aware of a nagging apprehension. Had I been too rash? Perhaps I shouldn't have volunteered. Maybe it was dangerous. But I trusted the Verdants; no harm would come to me. And yet, and yet . . . I could always back out in the morning.

I got up from the bed, at which moment the light came back to full illumination, and stepped into my slippers. I absentmindedly picked up the remote control from the bedside table—some habits never change—then tossed it back. Perhaps a little stroll might help. Even as the thought entered my head, the door to my room slid into the bulkhead, and I stepped out into the corridor. I could see several hundred yards in either direction before the hall curved away from view.

As several Verdants went about their business, I caught sight of Tony and Megan walking toward me arm-in-arm about 50 feet away. They spotted me at about the same time, and Tony gave me a wave, which I self-consciously returned. He seemed to whisper something into Megan's ear, and she squealed with laughter, then gestured animatedly with a high-five in my direction.

"Sleep tight. Don't let the space bugs bite," she called out, followed by another squeal of laughter.

Both of them turned into a nearby room and disappeared behind the closed door. If I hadn't known better, I would have thought they were drunk. I returned to my room and eventually dozed off.

the probe

"Rise and shine, sleepyhead."

I opened my eyes and found Gina looking down at me. For a moment I forgot where I was. In none of my previous sleep breaks on either visit to the great ship had anyone ever entered the room to actually awaken me. They were great sticklers for observing my privacy. I wasn't offended, though, because Gina and I had developed a close enough attachment to safely break what I considered to be protocol in these matters. I would never consider her presence intrusive under any circumstance.

The Verdant in charge of the food cart, however, would

not feel comfortable in taking the same liberties, and so she waited outside the door until it was appropriate to enter. As usual, breakfast was a sheer delight, a veritable reproduction of a typical earthling's ultimate morning buffet.

"I hope you don't mind that I entered without your permission," Gina apologized. "It's just that you were oversleeping a bit and the hour is getting late."

"Not at all," I assured her. "I'm glad you did. You are welcome at any time. What time is it anyway?"

"The time is 04738.223." She was teasing again and probably smiling in her own inimitable Verdant way. "About 9 a.m. by your clock," she continued. I knew by this time that she possessed a playful sense of humor, and it wouldn't surprise me to learn that the numbers she had thrown at me were probably meaningless and really didn't represent any kind of star time. It likely was just a random string that served as the set-up for her little joke.

It occurred to me that I never saw a clock or anything vaguely resembling one—at least anything that I was familiar with—during my two visits aboard the ship. It probably wouldn't have mattered, though, as the Verdant concept of time is far more complicated than ours. (See Appendix 1.)

The food cart attendant left just as Clarence entered.

"Almost ready?" he asked.

I quickly finished my meal, brushed my teeth, shaved and showered, and again allowed myself the luxury of stepping into fresh garments, even though the ones that I had put on the night before were perfectly adequate to keep wearing. Just as I found on my first visit aboard, the drawers in the vanity contained a stack of neatly folded clean robes, a supply of fresh white T-shirts and boxer shorts, and several pairs of slippers identical to the ones that I was wearing. The underwear appeared to be cotton and was white. The robes were of a variety of pastel shades, which the Verdants seemed to favor, and the material was lightweight and smooth, yet had a sturdiness about it that seemed to belie the flimsy look of it.

The room Clarence led me to was about 1,800 square feet in size. It was the first time in either of my visits aboard that I saw pictures of art on the wall. The hues and tones were like nothing I had ever seen before, and beautiful beyond description. If they represented any particular forms, I could not identify them, but just gazing at each unique image had a mood-altering effect, evoking pure tranquility. Strange, muted music definitely not of an earthly variety filled the room almost on a subliminal level and added to the effect. The sounds were rapturous and inspired feelings that bordered on bliss. The mood was almost spiritual, as I was coming to understand the word, but definitely not religious.

A simple padded couch sat in the middle of the room, and beyond that stood a machine perhaps five feet tall and boxlike, containing a console of lights, some blinking while others burned steadily. Suspended above the box but still attached to it was a disk about six inches in diameter, from whose center projected a narrow cone with the point aiming outward. A series of rectangular multicolored lights encircled the disk, and four longer lights of different colors traversed the cone from base to tip. Another mysterious boxlike affair sat off to the side.

I was told to lie on the couch. Gina took my right hand between hers. A gesture of reassurance? However well intentioned, it was unnecessary because I was completely at peace, lacking even a hint of anxiety.

"Before we get started," Clarence said, "let me explain to you what you can expect. Once we begin the probe, your mind will go blank, although you'll be completely conscious and will experience absolutely no discomfort. You might experience some memories from different times in your life, but they will be fleeting. And they will be regressive, beginning with more current ones and then coming from earlier and earlier periods in your life."

That would be the effect of the probe as it penetrated and then transcended the memory banks of my current existence, he explained. It's also possible that no memories would be stimulated during this process. Once the probe delved into that area of the brain where no memories theoretically should exist, it would make a comprehensive search for anomalies.

The odds of finding any such irregularities were infinitesimal under most circumstances, he said. There was a slightly higher chance in my case, however, because there is some belief in reincarnation in human culture. In addition, some human individuals had tested positive.

"What will I feel if something does turn up?" I asked.

"You will experience snatches of strange memories that will appear to be completely alien to you. It will almost be like you are in someone else's body or mind. The retrieval recorder over there"—he pointed to the small box-like affair—"will chronicle the aberrations electronically, after which the data will be analyzed."

No electrodes, wires, or clamps would be attached to my skull. Nothing would actually touch me. The probe itself would do all of the work from the few feet of distance that separated me from it.

And then my mind went blank. I thought of nothing, but lay in complete comfort and brain stillness. Whoa! There was a flash of memory. I was already back in my 20s. A girl whom I had a crush on in college laughed and told me to get lost when I asked her for a date. That's a memory that I could live without. Then it was gone just as quickly—a blank mind again. . . . Pow! Another momentary recollection, this time from when I was seven. My mother was standing at the console radio in the living room weeping softly as the news of the attack on Pearl Harbor blared out. Then it was gone and my mind was again empty.

Minutes seemed to pass, although in my state of suspended cerebral activity there was no way that such an estimate could be trusted. It might have been seconds, it might have been hours. (After the session, I determined that it had been more than a few seconds but well short of several minutes.) And then I disappeared! Not physically, not literally. But I wasn't me anymore—I was somebody else. And I was no longer lying on a couch in a spacecraft moored in space behind the moon. The memories were sometimes vivid, rich in detail, other times obscure and nebulous. They flashed through my mind like a mental kaleidoscope, a constantly changing landscape of form and structure, each image revealing a different pattern, a different set of circumstances, but never coalescing into a recognizable whole picture.

By the time the session was over, I had thousands of pieces of a gigantic jigsaw puzzle whose picture might have consisted of millions of them. For instance, my name was

Charley. I had a bevy of brothers and sisters, was raised in a dirt-poor family, was born in 1904, and had no memory of anything after 1934. There were countless other snippets, but a very incomplete picture. I had no idea what to make of them. (I did retain many of the memories after the probe was concluded, and even to this day the memories that were stimulated continue to trigger more recollections that constantly add to my storehouse of knowledge about the previous life that I may have led.)

Both Clarence and Gina were intrigued.

"Well, you proved to be a very rewarding subject," he said. "Let's see what the analyzer has come up with."

Every aberrant memory was sorted into chronological order and gave a rather patchy biography of someone who either was a real person whose life I inhabited previous to my own, or who was merely a figment of my own imagination, depending upon one's perspective and belief systems. I was given an actual printout of the results, which ran to several thousand words. It was printed in English on a strange material that bore no resemblance to paper. It was white like any ordinary sheet of paper, but the printed words in black type seemed to leap from it with great clarity. It was very smooth to the touch, almost nonporous, yet it was easy to handle and was very resistant to crinkling. I got the impression that if I crumpled a page up in my hand and tossed it aside that it would rebound to its original form without a crease in it. However, I did not conduct an experiment to test that notion.

"What do you make of it?" I asked.

"As with all other such cases, we really don't know," Clarence answered. "On the surface, it appears that the memories construct the life of a rather insignificant individual who obviously had run-ins with the law and never amounted to much before his death. There are no memories after 1934, which probably indicates the year of death, although a comatose condition could also account for that."

As noted earlier, in cases where the memories indicated that the so-called reconstructed life might have been a prominent personage, a search could be initiated by feeding the information into the Verdant data banks that contain most of the history of the human species. Events in the lives of prominent people of the past that might correspond with the ostensible memories would then be scrutinized. Certainly it wasn't solid evidence, but it could serve as the basis for a reincarnation theory.

In my case, however, it was explained that it was unlikely that the public records would reveal any information to confirm the identity of the person that the aberrant memories represented. After all, if such a person ever did exist, he appeared to be just one of perhaps thousands of such nefarious characters of the time who went anonymously from cradle to grave. It was highly inconceivable that any connection could be made. Still, they said they would be willing to give it a try.

I graciously declined the offer, saying that I didn't want to put them to any bother, particularly when it appeared that the search would be fruitless. Nevertheless, I couldn't wait to read the report. I was anxious to see if it made some sense out of all of the bits of chaos swimming around inside my head.

In the report, the memories were arranged in the linear succession in which the incidents purportedly occurred, a structure that did not reflect my own recollection of events. That is, suspending one's disbelief for a moment and assuming that the memories actually represented a previous life, they were organized as they occurred during the reincarnated person's lifetime. Also, while most of the incidents that I recalled were primarily general in nature, the report augmented many of those memories with much greater detail.

For instance, I recalled one night when a couple of buddies and I (Charley?) broke into a store and burglarized it, but nothing more about it. The report from the analyzer indicated that we stole several cans filled with several hundred dollars in pennies. The store also served as a U.S. Post Office and the coins were the proceeds from the sale of postage stamps. Once I read that item, it triggered other memories and more details about the incident.

There was no doubt that the probe had uncovered something of significance—it turned out that some of the memories, both in the report and in my own recollection, did strike an odd chord of familiarity—but my skeptical nature would not allow me to presume that this was evidence of reincarnation. I wasn't going to dismiss the idea completely, but I needed much more convincing before I could accept such a theory. Perhaps the memories could be explained by something as simple as mere fantasy hidden deep in my subconscious. Perhaps they represented merely the germ of a story idea that, if left untouched, might have come bursting to the surface one day to become the basis for a novel.

The brain is a magnificently complex organ, and perhaps the probe itself somehow generated the memories, or possibly stimulated a portion of the brain that manufactured them out of nothing. I vowed to keep my mind open to any possibility, and thanked Clarence for taking me on such an adventure even if it hadn't really proved anything. I took the report with me as Gina and I left the room. She then reminded me that I wouldn't be able to take it back home with me, so if I wanted to digest it I would have to do so while still on the ship.

"You'd better do it now," she said. "There's a meeting that you have to attend in a couple of hours and then you and the other guests will be leaving."

"Already? It's been less than two days, hasn't it?"

She said the others had almost completed their business and were currently having lunch. One final session was scheduled that I was to attend, after which I would be returned to my home. I asked her about the nature of the meeting, but she replied that it would be explained to me at that time.

The moment of reckoning had finally arrived.

I didn't know what to expect. I was prepared for anything, yet I experienced no particular apprehension. I was simply gripped by a great curiosity and was resigned to whatever might come next.

I returned to my room and devoured the report, glad to have brought along my reading glasses.

the grilling

About two hours later, Gina came to my quarters and escorted me to a large room where my first impression upon walking in was that a bowling tournament could easily be hosted here and that the polished conference table was huge enough to double as a lane. I joined the 12 other humans whom I had met on my arrival. I include Paul in this number since he was in human form and none of the others knew him as anything but a mortal. There were also 15 Verdants present. Since I still didn't trust my ability to detect individuals, especially in a group this large, I scanned their name tags to see if Gus was among them. He wasn't there.

I certainly would have recognized Gina, but I knew she wouldn't be participating.

The only name I recognized was Martin, although I had no way of knowing at the time if it was the same Martin who had briefed me when I came aboard, the one with the attitude, the one to whom, if he were human, I would have felt no qualms in avoiding. We all sat at a large, round table that was capable of accommodating 30 or 40 people. The humans wore a variety of expressions, from seriously grim-faced to benignly indifferent to formally businesslike. The seating order was apparently random. I sat between a Verdant on my left and Lillian on my right. It soon became obvious that a Verdant female named Sarah would conduct the session.

"Let's get started," she said, and all conversation ceased. "We have a newcomer among us at this session, although you all know him and have met him. If you will bear with us I'd like to have Martin give him a short briefing about what has been occurring before we proceed with the business at hand."

Martin was seated almost directly across the table from me. He rose and looked in my direction.

"I discussed some of this earlier with you," he began. "All Ambassadors have been brought back aboard over the last few months to participate in some very serious business. In addition to presenting progress reports, they have also been engaged in discussions among themselves and with representatives of our species, specifically members of the Ad Hoc Committee for Coordination of Earth Contact. The committee, of course, represents the Intergalactic Federation of Sovereign Planets."

"I hope this doesn't take all day," I heard Carl mutter. He appeared to be agitated.

Martin turned to Sarah. She touched an index finger to her chin and said one word: "Blefus." Well, it sounded like one word to me but it could have been a phrase, a sentence, even a paragraph for all I knew about their language. The word was also delivered with a strange croaking sound.

"Of course," he said. "In a nutshell, we are troubled with the way things are going. Your Ambassadors have been brought back for high-level discussions, to express their opinions, to put forth arguments, and finally to be polled on whether they believe the time is still ripe to proceed, to keep the timetable on track. The people here today represent the final group of returnees. They also have been selected by all other Ambassadors as representatives to cast votes on one other matter that affects you personally. Do you have any questions?"

I sure did. I didn't like the sound of what I thought I had just heard.

"You're considering aborting the contact?"

Jim, the beefy guy whom I pegged as possibly a cop, piped up. "That's not at all what he said! He's talking about a possible delay, a postponement. He never said anything about abandonment." His tone was one of impatience.

"Hey, take it easy on the guy," Chip said. "He just asked a question and I think he's entitled to a civil answer."

"Why do we have to be so hostile?" Lillian interjected. "We've been at one another's throats almost from the time we came aboard."

"Ladies and gentlemen, please," Sarah said soothingly. "I think there has been enough anger, frustration, hostility, and bitter wrangling throughout our meetings. Let's try to conclude this final session on a positive note so that you can all leave as friends and colleagues united in pursuit of the cause."

"There are some among us," Martin went on, "and I speak of the distinguished guests in this room as well as officers in the IFSP, who are openly questioning whether we were premature in our overtures toward the people of Earth. Quite frankly, some of them are entertaining the possibility that we may have made a mistake. Personally, I find myself leaning in that same direction. Now that the conferences have essentially concluded, I have not been completely reassured."

Martin went on to explain that the Verdants raising the objections believe that humankind has not displayed the degree of progress that they had expected when the decision to make contact was made. They blame this alleged miscalculation on a misunderstanding of the depth of the diversity of the human race. In their opinion, further observation is required and they prevailed upon those in command to reassess whether the timetable should proceed as planned or whether it might be wise to delay it for a period of time.

"Is that question going to be decided here today?" I asked. "If so, I vote to proceed."

"Oh, sure, you would," Carl said. "You have nothing to lose compared to the rest of us. What important work have you done? None, that's what. You have absolutely no idea of how much effort has gone into the planning and preparation of this event. This is more than just a lark, which you apparently consider it. This is a monumental step in Earth's history. It must not, it cannot, be taken without consideration of the grave consequences that will result if it fails. The timing must be perfect."

I had chatted briefly with Carl at the social gathering and got the impression that he might be a scholar, a political scientist, but I never got any indication of the personal animosity he seemed to have toward me nor the passion that he was now displaying. I might have expected it from Hal because he and I hadn't exactly hit it off like bosom buddies.

"If the contact takes place prematurely and the negotiations break down because of an act of monumental stupidity, it could set the program back years, perhaps decades," Carl continued. "Believe me, I'm an expert on world politics, and I tell you that we have not been properly prepared for this event. In the beginning, I wholeheartedly supported the program and the timetable. But I have changed my mind. We are not ready."

Tom then jumped into the fray, claiming that while he respected Carl's viewpoint he could not agree with his conclusion. Every historical leap, every endeavor that advances humanity's frontiers, is fraught with risk and peril. The world would still be in the Stone Age if it weren't for the hardy and heroic individuals in every generation who were willing to challenge boundaries, who refused to accept limits, he said.

"Pioneering is not for the timid," he said. It was a mild rebuke and Carl took exception to it.

Lillian again protested the bickering, but Martin cut her off. "Let us proceed, ladies and gentlemen. Most of you are aware that there will be no vote today on this subject. The decision will be made in the months ahead exclusively by the Verdants after you all are back on your planet. Naturally, we will consider the counsel that the Ambassadors have provided us, and that will play a significant part in the decision."

Whatever the decision, he said, all Ambassadors will then be contacted and told whether to put their plans on hold or to proceed. Again, it was stressed that the decision is whether to delay the contact, not to abort it.

I didn't want to see lives put in danger, but I tended to side with Tom. Nothing ventured, nothing gained. If we adopt zero tolerance for risk, then time will stand still and nothing will be accomplished.

Paul was the only one who wasn't taking part in the discussions, but I got the impression that he was absorbing everything. Perhaps his role was strictly one of observer rather than participant.

"I'm confused," I said. "Martin enumerated these concerns earlier in a private discussion with me. But you (I was speaking to the Verdants) know our history, you are aware of the strife that has gripped the planet from the moment humans first appeared. We are a species of disharmony, struggle, and conflict. You knew that when you contacted us. But we have progressed in spite of those ugly and disagreeable traits that seem to be a part of our character. We have built a grand civilization and I think that humans, despite our obvious imperfections, are a noble species. I think we are ready."

There was a scattering of polite applause by both humans and Verdants. I was momentarily choked up, and had to stop for fear that my voice would crack. It had nothing to do with the show of support by the applause. Instead I felt a deep and disturbing burden inside my chest, and only with the greatest of effort was I able to stifle the sobs that lay just below the surface. I knew that if I allowed even one to escape, the floodgates would open and the rest would come pouring out.

I realized that I was grieving for my human brothers and sisters who populate our beautiful blue planet. They are good and gentle people, and yet they suffer so much because of the deeds of a small minority. We have so much potential and the universe holds so much promise, and I was sorely afraid at that moment that the promise was slipping through our fingers. It wasn't fair.

"I'll put it to you bluntly," Martin responded. "Things seem to be getting worse rather than better. We are disappointed that the righteous are not taking charge as we had anticipated they would. We are concerned that the corrupt are consolidating their forces of opposition and seem to be prevailing."

"He's talking about a grand conspiracy," Paul said, breaking his silence for the first time. "The word is out that the Verdants are here, but very powerful interests do not want them to be here. Events are being manipulated to discourage contact by showing that humankind should be feared and distrusted. Plainly speaking, it's a campaign of sabotage.

"They're telling us, or rather the Verdants, to go away."

"Can't you do anything about it?" I asked.

"You know we don't interfere in the domestic affairs of sovereign planets," Sarah said. "I tell all of you Ambassadors, as well as you, Deputy Envoy, that we are looking for more progress among the 80 percent than we have seen thus far. We are puzzled that this hasn't been happening. "And now, I think we have exhausted this subject. Let's move on to the final order of business."

A Verdant named Bruce then rose and addressed me in a tone that resonated as both official and decreed, as if he were reading from a bill of particulars although he had no reading material in front of him. Certainly it sounded prepared, if not actually rehearsed.

"Deputy Envoy, a delegation of Ambassadors has petitioned the Ad Hoc Committee for Coordination of Earth Contact to reevaluate your status as a member of the contact liaison team, to make a determination as to your suitability for performing the role for which you were recruited, and to take appropriate action, including termination of your services, in the event that a board of inquiry consisting of representatives of your peers and of the AHCCEC finds that you have failed to adequately and diligently represent the best interests of the Verdant-human contact effort."

That was quite a mouthful, and speaking of mouths, mine was simply agape as the full force of the words struck me.

"Members of your species who are here assembled, with the exception of the one called Paul, along with the panel of Verdants herein convened have been selected to act as that board of inquiry. The human members were chosen on the basis of a series of votes taken among all current Ambassadors to serve as their representatives in this matter, and the Verdant participants were conscripted as representatives of the Verdant High Command.

"Do you understand the nature of these proceedings?" Bruce asked.

"No, I don't," I replied. It was all I could muster at the moment and it was a colossal understatement. The fact is I was shaken to the core.

Over the last couple of years I had taken a lot of heat. Admittedly, I willingly became a public figure and, as such, made myself fair game for criticism from every imaginable quarter. I expected it and accepted it as a matter of course. I have no regrets.

Sniping from beyond the walls of the fort is one thing, but never during this period did I expect to be called on the carpet by the Verdants themselves nor the distinguished ladies and gentlemen who comprised the select group that I felt honored to be associated with. Did I understand the nature of the proceedings? No, I had no idea what was going on. I was overwhelmed by this completely unexpected onslaught. My emotions ran wild. I felt betrayed, besieged.

"What . . . what did I do?" I stammered. "How can . . . who . . . what is the complaint? Am I . . . being fired?"

"Take a deep breath," Paul advised. "Just relax."

I did, and it helped. According to Bruce, a number of Ambassadors—he didn't say how many, but enough to warrant a formal hearing on their petition—raised several issues of concern that they wanted addressed. I was to be given the opportunity to respond to each one. The board of inquiry would then determine whether my answers reasonably and satisfactorily put the issues to rest. If they did, the matter would be dropped. If they didn't, the panel had the discretionary authority to take several courses of action, ranging from merely offering me some cautionary advice to asking for my resignation.

These were my alleged "crimes":

∞ Gratuitously including in the book the sexual incident with Gina, which created the potential of bringing disrepute upon the program.

∞ Gratuitously including in the book an episode with a Verdant known as Minister Jason—which had the potential of offending the religious beliefs of a vast number of readers.

∞ Failing to conduct myself in the most dignified maner at all times by occasionally being flippant in public forums and in media interviews, which had the potential of causing audiences, readers, and listeners to conclude that I did not take the program seriously.

∞ Admitting to readers who had contacted me in person and via letters and e-mail that my mind was open to the possibility that my experience may not have been based in reality but rather could have been some form of delusion, mind control, or some other variable, any one of which had the potential of planting doubts in the minds of the public.

∞ Making disparaging remarks to several readers who contacted me by letter or e-mail seeking clarification of certain elements in the book or requesting addtional information. Some of these communications actually came from Ambassadors themselves, I learned.

∞ Failing to engage critics, doubters, and debunkers in spirited debate, thus giving them reason to infer that I had no defensible arguments and was acceding to their points of view, however erroneous those postions might be.

I looked around the room. Chip, Mary, and Tom

appeared to be allies. Paul was neutral, of course. I had already felt Hal, Carl, and Jim's hostility. Beverly was an uncertainty, although she was Hal's wife, so I suspected that she probably would side with him. Ditto with Lorraine, who was married to Carl. I considered Megan, Tony, and Lillian as on the fence. It also occurred to me—ironically so, given the discussion of that first night—that the group consisted of 12 people (counting Paul), the exact number that usually makes up a human jury. As for the Verdants on the panel, I had no idea what positions they would take.

Following are the highlights of the conversations that took place over the next several hours. For the sake of brevity, I have eliminated most of the extraneous comments, which consisted of reactions of disagreement or support for the arguments and counterarguments. However, I have included some, but not all, of the insignificant asides, quibbling, and petty personal remarks, opinions, and wisecracks. They did nothing to advance the proceedings, but they do help to characterize some of the participants.

"Why did you feel the need to include the explicit sexual incident with Gina in the book?" Lorraine asked. "I can't see that it served any positive purpose, and in fact even trivialized the message that you were supposed to deliver."

"I included it because it happened and I didn't feel that I had the right to censor any of the events that occurred," I said. "I think it helped to give a complete picture of my total experience aboard. I think it even humanized the Verdants, if I can use that contradictory analogy, allowing the citizens of Earth to relate to them, to better understand them, to help allay any fears or suspicions about them. I was embarrassed to write about it, but if there's one thing that humans can relate to, it's sex. As Jim so frankly pointed out, we are, after all, sexual beings."

"I can relate to that," Megan said with an impish smile. Tony nodded in agreement as the two exchanged glances.

"What about that religious business?" Jim asked gruffly. "You certainly must have been aware, even as an atheist, that large segments of the population probably would be offended, and rightly so, by its inclusion."

This was in reference to a chapter in *The Contact Has Begun* in which I reported that the Verdants practice a religion that is fact-based rather than faith-based, as human religions are. Some readers took the position that I was somehow challenging their own religious beliefs and practices. How they arrived at that conclusion is a mystery to me, but religion by its nature is a very emotional subject. As such, it often stirs passions that can preclude rational debate.

"I meant no disrespect to anyone or to any religious creed," I replied. "I certainly didn't mean to offend. But that incident did happen, and after much soul-searching, if you'll forgive the irony of that statement, I felt that I had a duty and an obligation to report the events as truthfully and as accurately as they occurred. And I still don't think it was inappropriate or disrespectful to include it."

I looked for some sign on Paul's face, but his expression remained totally neutral.

"Besides, too many devout religious types march stiffly and joylessly through life, always quick to take offense at anything that deviates from their own narrow and pompous views. They ought to lighten up a bit, maybe think more about sex and less about sanctity. Some of the men might even consider a session with Gina."

Mary snickered.

"See, that's a very good example of one of the objections that was raised about you," Carl groused. "We're engaged in a very serious historic undertaking, and you continually make flippant remarks. You don't seem to understand the critical nature of what's at stake. You make wisecracks at the most inappropriate times."

"Oh, lighten up," Chip said. "He's just joking around. Where's your sense of humor? Maybe the world would be better off if people threw more wisecracks around and fewer bombs."

"There's a time for joking and a time to be serious," Carl said haughtily.

"I plead guilty to not taking myself too seriously when conditions warrant it," I said. "In order to do that, it's necessary to be able to laugh at yourself. Can you do that?"

"He doesn't need to be able to laugh at himself—there are probably plenty of others who do it for him," Tom said good-naturedly. Carl was fuming.

"Enough, please," Sarah cut in. "It's getting too personal again."

"Why," one of the Verdants asked, "would you lead people to believe that you are not totally convinced that your experience was real? Doesn't that create doubts in their minds and make the jobs of the Ambassadors even more difficult in overcoming resistance when the time for consummating the contact finally arrives?"

"I have always maintained in media interviews and in speaking before public gatherings, as well as in my responses to letters and e-mail messages, that all of my sensory impressions tell me that my experience was real. However, a number of readers have suggested alternative explanations for my adventure, and I think it would be presumptuous and arrogant on my part to stubbornly insist that only my version has validity.

"What I have said is that I continue to have an open mind and that anything is possible, but until someone can offer a reasonable, rational alternative explanation that I can accept, I would continue to trust my sensory impressions, which tell me that the events that I described in the book are real. Of course, being here now has removed any doubt in my mind, and I will hereafter state unequivocally that there is no alternative explanation. This is real. I am now totally convinced of that."

"I may not like his other positions, but I'm a scientist of sorts," Carl said. "And a good scientist always has an open mind. When the mind closes, then the scientist fails his calling. So I agree wholeheartedly with the Deputy Envoy on this particular issue. I still think that certain of his other behaviors erect obstacles that we Ambassadors are going to have to overcome when the time for contact approaches. It will make our task that much more difficult."

"I agree with my husband," Lorraine volunteered.

"Derogatory remarks to interested parties who seek information is not exactly the diplomatic way to win converts," another Verdant said. "That seems to be counterproductive and also tends to create resistance. How do you explain that, Deputy Envoy?"

"Your species has repeatedly expressed amazement at the diversity that exists among the 6 billion or so individuals who comprise the human species," I replied. "Some people are just jackasses, and I think I'm more qualified to identify them than you are. I can read between the lines. I am better equipped to determine if a statement should be taken literally or if there are nuances, hidden agendas, or subtle implications that mark them as disingenuous. There can be tremendous hostility, maliciousness, and insincerity behind what appears to be an innocent and benign comment or question.

"I don't claim to be any more astute than the average person, but I spent 30 years in the newspaper business and I usually can tell if I'm being misled. Verdants don't lie or engage in deception. Humans do. And as the old saying goes, it takes one to know one.

"I have never knowingly made an insulting remark to anyone who wasn't asking for it. If that's a crime, then fire me."

I was getting tired and impatient. If they wanted someone else for the job, that was fine with me.

Nevertheless, I went on to explain that critics, doubters, and debunkers as a rule have no sincere interest in becoming better informed. They simply have preconceived notions to which they stubbornly cling and will challenge any statement, theory, idea, or thought that does not rigorously conform to their own myopic perceptions. In essence, all they want to do is argue, and their minds are so tightly closed that engaging in conversation with them is akin to talking to a mule.

In addition, because a number of rational and sincere people made some valid and reasonable points in suggesting that my experience might not have been as cut and dried as I remembered it—and because I respected their opinions—I chose not to argue my point of view with them zealously. Thus, I told the panel, I adopted the attitude early on that I had no interest in trying to convince or persuade anybody of anything and I refused to be drawn into debate over the issue.

The meeting lasted about two hours, and when I indicated that I had nothing further to say in my defense, Bruce said, "Thank you, Deputy Envoy. You are excused." With that, Gina entered the room and escorted me out while the rest of the participants remained seated around the table.

"I thought you handled yourself quite well," she said as we returned to my quarters.

"You heard what went on?" I asked.

"Oh, yes, heard and saw. I watched the proceedings in an anteroom. Along with a couple of thousand others, I might add."

As for myself, I felt betrayed in that I had put my reputation and credibility on the line by going public and that this sacrifice was not fully appreciated by some of those involved. Yet I was out in the open to be sniped at by those who had not made a similar commitment to revealing themselves. This angered me. I felt testy and, quite frankly, I was in the mood to tell them I was washing my hands of the whole affair. I can't say that I was consciously considering it at the moment. But I was in the mood.

Back in my room, I spent about an hour studying the deep-probe analysis report, talked with Gina for about another hour, and then a food cart was wheeled into the room. A half an hour later, Gina asked me for the probe report and told me to change into my personal clothes. She then ushered me back to the meeting room.

"Deputy Envoy," Bruce began after I had taken my seat, "it is my pleasure to inform you that a majority of the members of the board of inquiry, after due deliberation and a vote of all members present, has found that the allegations contained in the complaint against you are without merit and that you will continue to serve as a Deputy Envoy if you so desire. The board further, by majority vote, wishes to extend to you its thanks for the services you have thus far rendered, regrets any anxiety that you may have suffered as a result of these proceedings, and offers its heartfelt condolences for the discomfort that you have endured as a result of your unselfish devotion to duty in serving the interests of the Verdant/human agenda.

"The board also, by majority vote, would like you to consider serving as chief spokesperson for the Verdants among your people. We will understand if you decide not to accept."

I was flabbergasted. There was so much to absorb that my head started spinning, and not a sound in the room as I tried to sort it all out. I finally boiled it down to two sentences: I wasn't being fired, and they were offering me more responsibility. I understood the first part, but the second part left me with a lot of questions. What do you mean, I asked, by serving as your spokesman. What am I expected to do? Send out press releases? Arrange speaking engagements?

"It's largely ceremonial," Bruce explained. "There are no real duties involved. When we begin making formal announcements to the people of Earth as the day of contact draws near—whenever that is—we will funnel all information of a general nature through you if you choose to accept the position. Of course, there will be times when specific

Ambassadors will be required to make announcements that are duty-related. But you would be our spokesperson for all other information that we want released."

In one sense it was a dream come true: to remain a key participant in this incredible moment in humankind's history. And I truly felt honored by their show of support, grateful for the privilege of having been offered such a role.

But the previous two years had taken their toll. I felt drained in body and spirit from the demands that had already been placed on me; to take on even more seemed daunting. With so much on the line I didn't want to make mistakes, and wondered if someone younger would be more appropriate. But then I remembered how I felt when I thought of my fellow human travelers and how most of them deserved a better life. So I tentatively agreed, but reserved the right to step away at any time.

"Good enough," Sarah said, and then most of the people in the room, including all of the Verdants, rose and approached me. Each Verdant bowed slightly and said, "Congratulations." Chip, Paul, Megan, Tony, Mary, Tom and Lillian shook my hand and offered their good wishes.

Right before I left the ship, I asked Gina one more time if any major decisions had been made between the Ambassadors and the Verdants.

"Only one decision is under consideration, and it hasn't yet been made. The Ambassadors gave our people their input, our people listened, and the High Command will make a choice sometime in the near future."

"What do you think it will be?" I asked.

"I don't know and I'm not at liberty to speculate. I do have a bit of advice for you, though. Maybe it can be your first official announcement as our spokesperson."

She paused.

"Get your act together. There are grave concerns that have permeated up to the highest levels."

"My act?"

"No, humans'."

An ominous farewell. Then in a breath I was gone, back in my bedroom. It was Martin Luther King Day.

epilogue

When a couple of years slipped by after my initial visit to the *Goodwill* without further word from the Verdants, I resigned myself to the likelihood that I was out of the loop and that my assignment had been completed. Intellectually, I could understand the logic behind such a decision: My job had been a fairly simple one and I was probably one of the least important players in the unfolding drama. Still, psychologically and emotionally, the realization left me with a strange feeling of emptiness.

But when I began suspecting that some of the extraordinary dreams I was having were some form of communication, when I experienced the breakthrough episode of intuitive clarity that eventually led me to Paul and Chip, I felt a renewal of hope. And then when Gina knocked on my door, my spirits soared again.

However, while I could imagine many wonderful scenarios that would have led to my return, I never once considered that the reunion might take place under the dire circumstances that demanded it. I was thrilled to go back, but I couldn't rejoice over the reasons that prompted it.

But that's all over now and the final decision on contact is in other hands. All humankind can do now is wait.

Ironically, even knowing that those of us who have been personally involved in initiating the contact could face a grievous disappointment as a golden opportunity slips through humankind's fingers, there also comes a certain sense of relief. By resigning ourselves to fate, by surrendering to whatever destiny awaits us, a great burden has been lifted from our shoulders. We have done our duty to the best of our abilities, and if we lose it will not be because of lack of trying.

I speak, of course, for those involved, for those who have accepted roles to play, for the recruits of all standing. I do not mean to imply that the human species as a whole should not continue the struggle that one day will lead to recognition and acceptance as equals in the cosmic community.

On a personal note, I still am optimistic that the contact will take place as scheduled. However, at this point I am not certain what that schedule is. As I noted earlier, I received it secondhand through X, the former Ambassador recruited from the *Times*. But his disappearance from the picture, and the obvious fact that Verdants such as Martin are in dissent about the wisdom of contact at this time, throws an unknown quantity into the equation.

At a minimum, I believe that the Verdants want to deliver a wake-up call, to shake us out of our complacency. What better way to inspire us to renew our commitment, to call upon our inner reserves of strength and spirit, than to challenge the 80 percent to take control of the Earth's destiny, as a prelude to the historic summit with the Verdants?

This would appear to be a clever bit of reverse psychology. How many thousands of coaches in untold numbers of athletic contests have resorted to the same halftime tactic to reach the hearts and minds of their players?

I also cannot believe that a species so intelligent and technologically advanced is capable of such a gross miscalculation no matter how baffled they admit to being over the maddening complexity and diversity of the human species.

And then there is the paradoxical matter of my being

offered the position of official spokesperson, supported by a majority of human and Verdant representatives. If there was even a remote possibility that the Verdants planned to pull back—even temporarily—it seems logical that the process of naming me or anyone spokesperson would have been deferred until a final decision on contact had been made. Otherwise, it would be a meaningless gesture and I don't believe that the Verdants engage in such senseless acts.

Bottom line? Take Paul's advice. *Pray*.

appendix:

Verdant Lifespans and Time Measurement

Another thing I learned from Paul is that there is virtually no variation in individual life spans among the Verdants. That is, they live exactly 19,877 to 19,880 Earth years. The three Earth years differential is insignificant when compared to the total life span.

A Verdant year is equal to approximately 1,000 Earth days, give or take 10 days. However, while the Earth day is 24 hours long, the Verdant day is about 55 Earth hours long. So in 1,000 Earth days, or very roughly one Verdant year, there are 24,000 Earth hours.

For matters of simplification, let's use exactly 1,000 Earth days to the Verdant year and precisely 55 hours to the Verdant day. Based on those figures, there would be 436.363636 Verdant days to their year. That is, their planet would make one complete revolution on its axis 436.363636 times during the time that it takes for it to make one orbit of their sun. In that same time, the Earth would revolve on its axis 1,000 times. On Earth, 55 hours would pass during each revolution of Verdant on its axis.

Trying to compare Earth time with Verdant time is too complicated for me to understand, but Paul seemed to have no problem with it. He did say that there are 36 time zones on Verdant, whereas there are 24 on Earth. From each zone, we humans get a time measurement that we call an hour. Then we break those hours down into smaller units called minutes and seconds.

Paul never did mention what the Verdants call the

measurements from each of their 36 time zones. However, like humans, they also break those time units down into smaller and smaller components.

Also, methods of measuring time vary from planet to planet and species to species because of the different rotation and revolution periods as the worlds make their orbits and turn on their axes. Even Verdant time measurement varies from colonized planet to colonized planet and differs from the home-planet time.

There is, however, a standard universal time measurement system that all species use when traveling in space, Paul said. Presumably, humans will also have to learn how to tell universal time once they become star travelers.

part 2
Reporter's Notebook

I am a diarist, a prodigious note-taker—a habit that I picked up during my newspaper career. A pen and notebook have been my constant companions for 40 years and I rarely go anywhere without them. When it's impossible or inconvenient for me to tape-record or jot down material that strikes me as noteworthy, I jump onto the computer at the earliest opportunity—in prior years it was the typewriter—and enter it into my journal when the information is still fresh in my mind

In the last few years, the time that I have sat before the computer compiling my notes has increased spectacularly, not a surprising development considering the extraordinary events in my life during that period. Much of the material from my journal has found its way into this book, but the bulk of it languishes there unseen and unread by anyone but myself.

Although it is not vital to the telling of the story you have just read, nevertheless I find some of it to be entertaining, instructive, informative and insightful. While the following material did not find its way into the main text of the book, it did provide valuable background, helped me keep my perspective, guided me in organizing the book into readable form, and aided me in establishing a consistent tone.

I would now like to open up some of the more interesting pages of the notebook for the readers' perusal and offer you the following vignettes, anecdotes, observations and reflections.

Sunday, April 26, 1998

My wife and I drove to San Francisco to attend a talk by Dr. Doreen Virtue, an author of numerous bestselling books on angels with whom I had exchanged e-mail messages. I had never met her personally, but something about her, her books, and her messages intrigued me enough that I was willing to make the 700-mile round-trip drive to attend her lecture.

At one point during her presentation, she asked the audience if anyone could see the guardian angel that she said accompanied her at all times. A smattering of people raised their hands, and I was not one of them.

I looked around the room. There I sat, a mainstream journalist who had nevertheless abandoned his past and who now found himself in a seminar on angels being held in a crowded room at something called the Whole Life Expo, in a convention hall jam-packed with what appeared to be thousands of people. And these weren't the type of straitlaced people with whom I normally associate.

But since I can now be classified as an oddball myself, at least from a mainstream perspective, I am more kindly in my judgments of others who have iconoclastic views and interests.

It's astounding how ignorance can be so blinding. Once I was able to see beyond the foolishness of my own bias, to see the individuals rather than the group, I beheld such interesting, fascinating, unusual characters that I felt privileged to be among them. I regretted the lifetime of condescending isolation during which I kept such people at arm's length. How many extraordinary people I did not meet as a result of my haughty ways will never be known.

Some hours later, in the middle of the vast emptiness of the San Joaquin Valley, as we hurtled homeward on Interstate 5, I casually turned to my wife and asked, "Did you see it?"

"What?" she said, turning to look out of the side window.

"No, not out there. The angel," I said. "Did you see the angel that Doreen was talking about."

"I'm afraid not," my wife responded.

"Me, either," I said, and we drove in silence for most of the remainder of the trip back home, stopping once for gas and for food.

But I *had* seen it. It had been standing behind her, towering at least a foot over her, perhaps 6 feet 6 inches to 7 feet tall, an ethereal form in human shape that was paradoxically visible and yet transparent. When I first became aware of it, I stared transfixed, and my breathing became shallow. No gasps of surprise came from the audience, which puzzled me and caused me to consider the possibility that I was perhaps hallucinating, or that I had somehow gone into some sort of hypnotic trance. After all, the room was stifling hot, not only because the weather was warm but also because of all the body heat that the crowd was radiating.

The conditions were ideal for lulling a body into a state of soporific stupor. If I recall, either the air-conditioner was not working or there was none—it being San Francisco, and all—and a series of fans labored vainly and feebly to stir an occasional whiff of breeze out of the sultry air. I had looked at my wife for some sign of confirmation, but saw none.

I really didn't want this to be happening. It was too

uncanny for me. It seemed that I had been lurching drunkenly through life for the last year, and just when it seemed that I was getting my bearings again, some other extraordinary event would come along and destabilize me.

Well, I was going to sit on this little incident. I wasn't going to say anything to anybody, at least not until I got some answers, until I understood if these things were real or if perhaps I was going crazy.

I stared at the figure behind Dr. Virtue, making an effort to study the eyes, the nose, the mouth, the shape of the face, but the more I stared the more I realized that I couldn't really focus on any part of the figure. I was getting an impression rather than a sharp picture. I soon discovered that if I looked slightly off center of the figure, using my peripheral vision, I actually got a much clearer view of it.

After her lecture, Dr. Virtue worked her way through the crowd, making her way downstairs to an authors' table where she autographed copies of her books. The guardian angel stayed right with her.

I was drenched in sweat by the time my wife and I got out of the building, and there was no doubt in my mind that there was more to my profusion of perspiration than the mere heat of the day. I was emotionally rent.

I have never mentioned the incident to anyone, which has to be one of the more incongruous decisions of my life considering that I had stood up before the whole world and proclaimed that I had had contact with extraterrestrial beings. And yet I shied away from telling anyone that I had witnessed an angel. Certainly more people believe in angels than in space aliens and would be more receptive to giving credence to an account of the former than of the latter. I have no scientific evidence to back up this belief, but I hold it firmly if for no other reason than the empirical evidence that builds with observation and experience.

Think about it. How would others react if you told someone "I saw an angel last night" versus "I saw a space alien last night"? I'm pretty sure that people would think you had been blessed in the first circumstance and that you were daft in the second. How paradoxical that I could admit to being abducted by space aliens and yet was incapable of finding the courage to confess that I had seen an angel. The Verdants are right: We humans are a very strange species.

August 1998

While I was delivering a talk at the 2nd Annual Summer Seminars of the International UFO Congress in Laughlin, Nevada, one of the people who approached the microphone posed an enticing proposition.

The questioner asked me if I would like to be introduced to two Ambassadors who were in the room. I hesitated. On the one hand, I was consumed by a burning curiosity to meet them, to learn their identities, to discuss their experiences to see how closely they paralleled mine. On the other hand, my cautious nature raised a red flag that warned me that such disclosure might be premature, that perhaps I should wait to see if the Verdants would approve. Since the unscheduled meeting with X and John at my house in April, I was really swimming in uncharted waters. I thought that perhaps the information that was offered was something that I shouldn't be privy to at that time.

I equivocated as I pondered the question. Finally, I decided to err on the side of caution, and I declined the invitation. But I sure was interested, and it took every shred of my resolve to turn down the opportunity. I also had to give very serious consideration to the possibility that someone might be playing a joke on me. Even worse, there was the remote possibility—I hadn't yet developed a keen sense of suspicion that one seems to need in this arena—that this might be a ploy to gain my confidence and lure me into confiding in them, revealing things that I shouldn't be talking about.

One day at Laughlin, before I had given my talk, I was sitting at my book table when a very large fellow approached me and began engaging me in conversation. He admitted to me quite frankly—and I judged by the tone of his voice and his gestures that he was complaining—that for 30 years he had been honestly convinced that he would become the primary spokesman for the aliens when they made their presence known to humankind.

"Now I find out that I don't even qualify as an Ambassador," he groused. "I don't have a college education, and I don't have the other background that you mentioned in your book."

He really seemed annoyed, and I instinctively tried to console him. First, I told him, my book did not say that all Ambassadors had to have college degrees. He was misreading it. The only time I mentioned a college degree as a qualification was in reference to the person the aliens would recruit to write their white paper. And that person would not be an Ambassador, but rather a Deputy Envoy.

Basically, the gist of his complaint was that he had

been active in the UFO community for three decades and that it just didn't seem fair that an "outsider" would be chosen over longtime loyal believers. He perceived it as some sort of betrayal on the part of the aliens by not rewarding that faithfulness.

I sympathized with him, and I truly understood his complaint. I suppose an analogous situation would be a company bringing in an outsider to fill an important management position instead of promoting a hardworking, dedicated employee from within. I can relate to the resentment that such a move could generate. I saw it happen at the *L.A. Times* again and again. There's a cynical bromide repeated in many offices across the nation to the effect that an expert is some guy who flies in from out of town. Ironically, the employee who is passed over in favor of the "expert" from out of town would be considered an expert herself if she applied for a position with a company in another city.

However, in my own defense, I tried to put the issue in a perspective that he could understand.

"Suppose the Verdants did select you to announce their intentions," I said. "Is anybody going to be surprised when you report that the aliens are coming? You've been standing on street corners, so to speak, for 30 years telling everyone who will listen that the aliens are coming. All who know you expect you to talk about aliens. That's been your pattern. They'd be surprised if you didn't talk about aliens. Then suddenly you find that the aliens have appointed you to spread the word. Is anybody really going to take you seriously at that point?"

He grudgingly acknowledged that I had a point and finally wandered away. A woman at another table had overheard the conversation, and she approached me when the large fellow left.

"He feels betrayed," she told me. "And he's not the only one. Others here are talking about you as that 'outsider,' and there's a lot of resentment."

I was dumfounded.

"You're kidding!" I said. I still had some capacity for being surprised.

It was a clannish mentality, but it was at work at the conference, she told me. Some people who have spent many years, perhaps a good part of their lives, studying, researching, investigating the UFO phenomenon can be quite antagonistic toward others whom they see as interlopers, Johnny-come-lately types jumping on the bandwagon. I suppose it's especially galling when that person is a former skeptic who has been derisive in the past of the field and the people in it.

I'm not sure I blame them. It does seem unfair, and if I were in their position I suppose I would feel the same.

But I didn't make the rules, so I left Laughlin with a clear conscience.

September 1998

I received an e-mail from a lawyer who represents a UFO-interest group that believes there is a government cover-up regarding extraterrestrials. He wanted to meet with me to discuss my experience. I thought I might be able to learn something, so I agreed, although not without some initial hesitation. I remembered the meeting I had had with X and John at my home the previous April. I had taken their advice to heart and raised my level of suspicions in my future dealings with people in general—strangers and acquaintances—alike. I had been operating on a higher alert status ever since in discussing my experience with others, and I vowed to proceed with caution.

I e-mailed back to the lawyer and said that I would be amenable to meeting him but that I had no knowledge of any government cover-up. That is not to say that such a thing might not be a reality, but I simply had no information. Also, I had an assignment, which I completed, and I am very wary of getting involved in any other activities that are not sanctioned, I told him. I have been under pressure from groups and individuals to do so, and I have resisted. I just think it's better that I tiptoe around very gingerly.

I had been scheduled to address a meeting of the MUFON chapter in Orange County (Anaheim), and he agreed to attend, after which we could have our discussion. However, when I phoned the MUFON chapter to get directions, I got an automated message indicating that another speaker was scheduled for the date in question, Wednesday, September 23.

I double-checked my date book and confirmed that I had blocked out that evening for the talk. Well, this was certainly an interesting turn of events, although I still don't know what to make of it. I wondered at the time if it was just a mix-up or if there were more machinations behind it than met the eye.

The lawyer was scheduled to speak at a meeting of the Art Bell Chat Club of the San Fernando Valley, so I attended his talk and then we went to a local restaurant afterward.

Fate had thrust me into this metaphysical, New Age, UFO arena, and sometimes I felt like Alice stepping through the looking glass. It was a fascinating, sometimes scary, place, and I had come into contact with some very strange—albeit interesting and intriguing—people and ideas. But if I thought that I had heard and seen all that this wonderland had to offer, I was being premature. For things were about to get "curiouser and curiouser."

The lawyer handed me a tiny plastic bag, approximately the size of a business card, that contained about half a teaspoon of what appeared to be gray ash. It had a sweet, perfume smell.

The packet was wrapped in a piece of paper on which were written seven words.

Invitation from Sai Baba
Puthaparti, India
—Vibhuti—

I learned later that Sai Baba is an Indian with a following of millions of devotees who believe he is an avatar. Well, there is no doubt that I was learning new things—and the meeting with the lawyer hadn't even begun yet.

The lawyer told me that I have information that his clients need to confirm their beliefs that I have been deceived and misled by the Verdants. His clients have been monitoring this particular species for some time, he told me, and they are convinced that the aliens are not as benevolent as I portray. Specifically, he said, the Verdants typically give assurances that they have great respect for the sovereignty of all other species, but that such declarations are disingenuous.

The Verdants are untrustworthy and deceptive, and use pledges of respecting sovereignty as a disarming technique to gain the confidence of the species with whom they are dealing, according to the beliefs of his clients, the lawyer told me. Once they have established a foothold, or beachhead, on the host planet, the Verdants furtively consolidate their power and resources to gain control over the planet and its inhabitants, according to the lawyer's clients. Puppet governments are then created, which are controlled by the aliens, and sovereignty is forfeited, the lawyer's clients believe.

All very interesting, but I hadn't yet seen his point. He said it was necessary for me to supply the names of the Ambassador from the *Los Angeles Times,* the human I met aboard the starship, and any names from the roster of Ambassadors that I could remember. I never did quite understand why he wanted this information, but I presume it had something to do with his lawsuits.

I smiled in amazement. I had to give the man credit. He certainly was forthright. I reminded him that I had no intention of getting involved in any lawsuits, nor would I take any action or speak any word that had even the remotest chance of compromising my position, and consequently the entire mission. I told him quite bluntly that I would never consider naming anyone unless I received incontrovertible authorization from—and here I nodded my head skyward—"high authority" to do so.

"Where do your loyalties lie?" the lawyer asked me quite sincerely.

So that's what it came down to, a choice between serving the aliens or the human race! Of course I would not betray my own kind if the question came down to choosing sides. But it quickly occurred to me that loyalty was not the issue, although that's the bait—which stirs the blood and inflames the spirits of all patriots—with which he almost snared me. It was a masterful bit of diversion.

I told him firmly that I disagreed with his clients, and that I thought they were wrong in their beliefs about the aliens. The Verdants are the most benevolent, kind, compassionate, ethical, moral individuals that I had ever met, I told him.

"I believe them and not your clients," I said, adding that any information they needed could be found in the book and that I had no additional data to supply them.

But he was persistent, claiming that I knew the names of many Ambassadors and that I had an obligation to identify them.

We must have spent a couple of hours in intensive debate, bantering, jockeying for intellectual position, quibbling over fine points, pontificating, poking at each other's arguments in search of weaknesses. Actually, I enjoyed the stimulation of the exchange and, in all fairness, I should point out that the conversation was friendly and mostly civil. He was passionate about his mission, and we were engaged in a clash of wills, but I liked the man. He even asked me to autograph his copy of my book, which I was pleased to do.

"How can you say that a species that kidnaps humans is benevolent?" he asked at one point.

I had wrestled with that moral and ethical issue myself privately on several occasions. Finally, I was able to reconcile those "unsolicited visitations" with my own value system by viewing them as a necessary ingredient for the common good. I know it's a bit feeble, but that's the best I could do.

Could that be interpreted as Machiavellian? Was I embracing that old bromide used by tyrants for centuries that "the end justifies the means"? It's a tough call, and even today it nags at me occasionally. But in those moments of doubt, I am reminded of an incident that happened some years ago when I was still working at the *Los Angeles Times*.

I had left the *Times* building at about 10:30 or so at night and was crossing Spring Street at 2nd Street on my way to the parking garage. Spring Street is one-way southbound, although there is one northbound lane dedicated to buses and emergency vehicles. As I approached the far curb, I almost stumbled over a man lying in the bus lane.

He was drunk and dirty, which was no surprise since Skid Row is but one block east on Main Street. He apparently had cracked his noggin when he fell because fresh blood was oozing out of a gash on his forehead. The traffic light had changed in the meantime, and a bus was rumbling down on us out of the darkness as I clasped my hands under his arms and around his chest. I hoisted him onto the sidewalk just as the bus roared by. He gazed up at me semi-consciously as I gently leaned him into a sitting position against a building.

It was the second time in my 25 years at the *Times* that I had pulled an intoxicated man out of traffic lanes. There is no doubt in my mind that both would have been killed if I had not happened upon them when I did, particularly since both incidents occurred in darkness. So I'll take two checkmarks to my credit for lives saved, please. Maybe someone is keeping score.

Technically, I told the lawyer, I abducted those men. I took them against their will, since both were asleep—if one can call a drunken stupor sleep—and moved them to a different place. The only difference is, I did not return them to the places in the street afterward. But morally, can my actions really be described as abductions? My motives were purely altruistic, and the action was in the best interests of the "abductees." I gained no personal advantage by my actions, and no interests of mine were served, except that I felt better as a human being. It was expedient for me to take them, and I have no compunctions about it. In these cases, the ends truly justified the means.

The lawyer countered good-naturedly that he objected to being compared to a drunk in the street who needs saving. He is quite capable of running his own affairs, making his own decisions without the intervention of some meddling third-party extraterrestrials to unilaterally determine what is best for him, thank you, he told me.

I explained to him that he will be as free after contact as he is now and that if he does not wish to participate in the cooperative effort between the two species, he will retain every unfettered right to make that choice. He will retain his individual sovereignty, just as the human race will retain its autonomy, I told him.

"Only those who wish to participate will do so. No one will be forced to do anything."

Up until this point, the repartee, the bantering, the arguments and counter-arguments were a stimulating game that I was enjoying. But then, during the only time in our genial conversation, an ominous note was thrown in. It momentarily wiped the smile off my face and caused me to consider the possibility that he might be able to really complicate my life, perhaps cause me big trouble. He could subpoena me, haul me into court to force me to divulge the information that he was seeking, he said.

I hesitated for only a moment and then told him with a twinkle in the eye that I thought that was a great idea. That means I would get a free airline ticket to Phoenix, or wherever, plus free meals and hotel accommodations. I was tweaking his nose good-naturedly.

"That publicity should sell a lot of books," I said, my jovial mood resurrected. "And then I still won't reveal the names."

"You'll be compelled to," he stated. I think he was enjoying the game as much as I was. Despite that one portentous comment about the subpoena, the entire conversation was cordial, a harmless jousting match.

I suggested that if I did reveal the names that he was seeking, there was a very real possibility that I wouldn't survive the experience. What did he think of that?

My death would be a small price to pay to save humanity from these alien creatures, he suggested quite frankly. It was a very logical and rational rebuttal, and I do appreciate reasoned argument free of sob-sister emotionalism. Nevertheless, he could have displayed just a tiny regretful pause before so quickly and enthusiastically volunteering my life for the greater good.

Anyway, I considered it a strictly hypothetical point since I don't buy his argument that the Verdants pose a threat to humans.

Suppose, I said, that I revealed the names of five Ambassadors who might be living in Libya, Iraq, Afghanistan, Iran, and some other country, and suppose they were all subsequently murdered or had simply disap-

peared, never to be heard from again, a la Jimmy Hoffa.
"Do you think I could live with that on my conscience?" I asked.

"Why would they be assassinated?" he asked.

"Because tyrannical leaders of outlaw nations are going to be deposed and lose their power if contact takes place," I responded.

The United States government is not going to kill someone from The *Los Angeles Times,* he said indulgently. That's probably true, but I pointed out that even if lives weren't put into jeopardy, the exposed Ambassador or Deputy Envoy could lose his/her effectiveness at the least, and possibly his/her job. In fact, I have been asked by several friends at the *Times* not to visit them at the plant out of fear that their positions could be jeopardized. I can understand those concerns. Certainly, tongues would begin wagging and false conclusions drawn from such an association.

Then we both gave our summations, he claiming that the aliens have nothing to gain by helping us, that they have ulterior motives aimed at eventual control of the human population, and that I have been duped into helping them to further their agenda. I countered that I have no reason to believe that the government is involved in a cover-up, that I must trust my own instincts and sensory impressions, and that I would never be able to forgive myself if the planned contact were disrupted because I had "outed" even one Ambassador.

In hindsight, I should have also pointed out to him that the primary reason the Verdants are here concerns interplanetary relations. As they do with all planets on the verge of space travel, they are monitoring our intentions—and, if need be—will prevent us from bringing weapons into space in accord with IFSP laws. Aside from that, we are on our own as a sovereign planet.

We parted on friendly terms. But he obviously went away from the meeting with a different perspective than I had regarding the discussion because he followed up with a report that was posted on the internet. I was not portrayed as the hero.

October 1998

The rumor mill is operating at peak efficiency. The critics are having a field day. And some readers have somehow gotten the strange notion into their heads that I have an abiding interest in reading long-winded—and often semi-literate—diatribes informing me how ignorant, misguided, and misinformed I am.

Well, I like to think of myself as open-minded, so I try to see the other guy's point of view and consider the possibility that he may be right. The important thing is to keep smiling.

I have made it a point to politely acknowledge the views of those who have written to me through letters or e-mail messages. I have personally answered, with only two exceptions, every letter and e-mail sent my way—not just the favorable ones but the critical ones as well.

One of the two exceptions involved a letter from a woman who took certain words in my book, rearranged the letters and came up with other words that she perceived as underlying messages, all of which she interpreted negatively. Such rearrangement is called an anagram.

Now I personally like words games myself, but looking at a "stop" sign at a street corner and mentally rearranging the letters to form the words *spot, tops, opts, pots,* and *post* hardly qualifies as a serious intellectual exercise or as legitimate scientific inquiry.

It took me about three seconds to discover that the letters in her name could be rearranged into the phrase "Jim dies hot." However, while that might be significant to some people, this "discovery" failed to get my heart beating faster with excitement, nor do I see any underlying message in it. In fact, it's quite meaningless. The reader found that the letters in Gwantelmipsa, the phonetic spelling of one of the Verdants' names, spells "a wet sampling" when rearranged.

Well, it's hard to argue with that conclusion. So I didn't. Of the hundreds of letters and e-mail messages that I have received, this one is hands-down the silliest. I think this reader could have a wonderful time if she ever discovered palindromes, words or phrases that are spelled the same backward and forward. A few that come to mind are:

A man, a plan, a canal, Panama.

Madam, I'm Adam. (An appropriate introduction by Adam upon meeting Eve in the Garden of Eden.)

Rise to vote, sir. (I heard this one on The Simpsons television show.)

The other letter that I opted not to respond to came from a TV producer who said that my book did an injustice to the alien research community. He didn't like what I had written, but rather than addressing the issues that were treated in the book he reserved most of his comments for assessing my shameful character. I have to admit that some of my former friends and colleagues would probably find him quite discerning. Nevertheless, it was quite evident that his hostility toward me was likely insurmountable and that there was little chance that we could open up a channel of communication in which we agreed to disagree. He said he couldn't understand how any respectable paper could have me on its staff.

I chose not to argue the point. I might not like my own conclusions on that subject.

Easter 1999

Chip, the Ambassador whom I had first met in the San Francisco Bay Area, spun an engaging little tale for me about his first visit to the *Goodwill*. Although I did jot down some notes a little later, and worked on an extensive and detailed account of our meeting that I typed into my computer when I returned home, it's impossible for me to quote him exactly. So I have taken literary license and compiled the following account as I remember it. The quoted material is only an approximation of the words spoken, and the text is mine, but the dialogue and text are an accurate portrayal of the events as he related them to me. Chip did not recall many names and simply referred to the various individuals anonymously and randomly.

The story picks up at a point during his orientation session when the meeting was shifted to a more informal setting after the aliens and Chip had gotten to know one another.

The leader of the group led them through a labyrinth of corridors, doorways and passages that finally took them to a cozy, secluded lounge area. It was an intimate, warmly decorated room, containing perhaps two dozen or so overstuffed armchairs scattered throughout and several fair-size pieces of furniture that we on Earth would refer to as coffee tables. It was well lit, but not uncomfortably bright. This was also the first and only time that he came across carpeting in the ship during his time aboard and it was luxuriant—something that probably would be very expensive in an exclusive flooring salon here on Earth. I personally never saw any carpeting when I was aboard.

Surprisingly for Chip, and for me when he revealed it, a large fireplace was built into one wall in which was burning what appeared to be standard wood logs. Much to his astonishment, wrapped around the fireplace from floor to ceiling and extending to encompass the two adjoining walls were shelves filled with what had to be thousands and thousands of books.

"Is that a real fire?" Chip asked no one in particular as the Verdants began arranging the chairs in a circle around one of the facsimile coffee tables.

"Very much so," one of the hosts replied. "It is strictly aesthetic, however, and serves no functional purpose for either heat or light. But most species that have mastered fire have what might be described as a spiritual bonding with it no matter how advanced their civilizations become."

Chip said he could relate to that easily enough, and I agreed with him. There is a coziness about a crackling fire that even humans continue to enjoy in the most modern of households where its only purpose is to warm the spirit. And what American—and presumably others—has not experienced seductive fascination while sitting around a campfire on a dark night, staring into the dancing flames?

They could have been in a reading room—a quiet place

of retreat—in a chichi country club adorning an exclusive neighborhood on Earth, if he hadn't known better, Chip said. I personally have never been in a country club because I'm just a simple working man, but if I had to imagine what such accommodations might look like, according to Chip's description, this was it. I failed to ask Chip if he had ever been in a country club. I would suspect he has because I got the impression that he earns a munificent salary. He followed their lead and sat down in one of the armchairs as the Verdants settled into their chairs around the table. All of them were introduced with Earth names, but Chip could remember only two or three of them.

"I suppose the books are strictly aesthetic, too?" Chip asked. "I mean, surely you must look upon them as a rather primitive way of storing information."

This probably was not an unexpected reaction by someone with Chip's background in computer technology.

"They are quite real," one of the female Verdants replied. "It's true that we can store every shred of knowledge that we have acquired over several hundred million years in a cyberspace package no larger than your typical Earth lawyer's briefcase. And, of course, we do have such storehouses of knowledge in abundance throughout the known universe."

All 650 trillion or so individuals who constitute the approximately 27,000 species that make up the Intergalactic Federation of Sovereign Planets have at their fingertips, in space or on planet, access to this store of knowledge through trillions of terminals interfaced with millions of mainframe computers. Whether fiction or nonfiction, every known written work in existence can be immediately accessed and read from a computer terminal.

"Then why . . . ?" Chip began.

"Because it's magical," the female said in anticipation of his question. "It's one thing to read an article, a nonfiction piece, or a novel on a computer terminal screen. When we simply want to extract knowledge, information, the computer is the most efficient method.

"But when we seek simple pleasure, reading just for the sheer enjoyment of reading—to hold the words in the hands, to feel the book against the flesh, to turn its pages, that is something that is spiritually soul-satisfying."

The thousands of books were mostly works of fiction, representing what was considered some of the greatest literary pieces ever written—the classics of the universe. Few individuals read technical manuals for pleasure, although there are some who do, Chip was told. But those volumes are stored mostly in vast libraries. This was a place of relaxation, of rest, a quiet place to escape into a good book for a few hours of distraction.

"Books are one of the first inventions of a civilized species, and yet—unlike such things as crude stone tools and primitive agricultural implements—they remain timeless," one of the aliens said. "No advanced civilization ever outgrows the love of books."

Chip told me that he, of course, would not be able to do any leisurely reading in this room since all of the books, he was told, were printed in the native Verdant language, of which there is only one, incidentally, unlike Earth's polyglot of tongues. The few books that he did examine confirmed that the books—at least the ones he opened—indeed were written in a language whose characters he had never seen before.

That was it. A simple and charming anecdote of a description of a room. No universal implications, no monumental secrets revealed. Perhaps one could gain from it a tiny glimpse into the complex, multifaceted Verdant character.

February 2000

I did follow through on my promise to myself to call the *Times* after my return from the ship and inquire whether X was still employed there. This satisfied a seductive curiosity on my part, but I can't in good conscience reveal what I learned because the information itself could be used to narrow down the list of potential candidates and make it easier for those who would love nothing better than to uncover the identity. I feel that would be a betrayal of trust, even though he is no longer speaking to me. If he is ever going to be identified, he is going to have to make the admission himself. I will have no part in it.

March 2000

I still don't know what to make of this reincarnation business. It's something that I've never believed in, and I wouldn't give it a passing thought even today if it weren't for the anomalous memories that purportedly were harvested from my brain. Any number of rational explanations might account for them, including fantasies, dreams, the germ of an idea for a novel reposing unacknowledged in my imagination. Also, as I said earlier, the probe itself might somehow have generated them, or possibly stimulated a portion of the brain that manufactured them out of nothing. Who knows? However, if there is such a thing as reincarnation, and if there is any validity to the concept that the memories represent a past life, I think I have a pretty good idea who that person was. All it took was a quick trip to the library to confirm my suspicions.

Glorious Diversity

I like the Verdants. They take some getting used to in trying to figure them out. Those seemingly impersonal, inexpressive faces belie the depth of the character and personalities hidden beneath them. But once you begin to know them, you can't help but recognize the wondrous intelligence, the delightful sense of humor, the gentle compassion, the loving concern for other beings, the selfless devotion to duty, the rock-solid discipline, the altruism, the purity of their moral and ethical standards, and a host of other admirable character traits that they all seem to possess.

I was talking to a man whom I had just met at a social gathering recently. He didn't know me and I didn't know him, but after a few minutes of small talk he had the audacity to tell me a joke with racial overtones. It wasn't a really vile, vicious story, but nevertheless it was in bad taste. I was upset because this man did not know me, and yet he was assuming that I shared his bigoted attitudes. I think that's what offended me most.

This was not a gathering of louts playing poker in the basement of the local meeting hall, or of loud-mouthed ignoramuses in a smoke-filled tavern. This was polite company, where such a joke should have been totally out of place.

He was a person of means, a leader in his community, a man of respect among his peers, a member of a business group, a churchgoer. I assumed that he even was a college graduate.

He grinned at me after finishing his story, and I simply stared stone-faced at him in astonishment.

"My God," I said, "do they still tell those jokes in Bakersfield?"

Then I turned and walked away in search of more genteel company. And yet, this man probably had no idea how offensive he was. In fact, I think he would be aghast if it were suggested to him that he was a racist or a bigot. He certainly was not the type who, in my opinion, would join a lynch mob, try to deny civil rights to minority groups, or engage in any other form of overt destructive behavior toward other racial, ethnic, or religious groups.

But would he engage in more subtle forms of discrimination? Would he favor white men over others in hiring, firing or promoting employees? What were his attitudes on welfare recipients, immigration, and other social issues? Would he buy a home in an integrated neighborhood? I don't know. But anyone who saw humor in the joke that he told, who would even relate such a story, whether in polite company or just a gathering of his "good ol' boy" pals at a local watering hole, is suspect in my mind.

What a shame, I thought at the time, that so many humans potentially would, and probably will, deny themselves the rich experience of associating with these marvelous creatures known as Verdants simply because they are different. But humankind's history is stained with such prejudice, a narrow-minded tribal mentality that breeds malevolence and distrust of others who are not of the same mold.

Intolerance is so spiritually self-crippling, and it's

difficult for me to understand how some people can inflict such damage upon themselves. Personally, I thrive and grow on the delightful and nourishing dish of diversity. It enriches me culturally, challenges me intellectually, and provides me with insights that enlighten and uplift me spiritually.

I not only like the Verdants, I also like Italians, African-Americans, Muslims, Irish, Jews, gays, blondes, old people, babies, Latinos, Robert DeNiro, Denzel Washington, Asians, and the woman who delivers my mail, among others.

Knowing that a certain element of humans would actually prefer not to associate with these wonderful extraterrestrial beings because of simple ignorance pained me. I found it sad that the Verdants would have to endure this absurdity on the part of a small segment of the human race.

I consider myself quite fortunate, actually, that I was never indoctrinated with the poison of intolerance that so many people willingly and mindlessly ingest in embracing certain religious dogma. Having no religion, I find myself quite incapable of harboring rancor against another person on the basis of his or her religious beliefs. The concept is so foreign to me, so . . . un-American.

Prejudice and intolerance of every stripe, be it based on race, ethnicity, political beliefs, gender, sexual orientation, socioeconomic status, skin color, immigration status, and a host of other superficial and meaningless differences is a crippling affliction of the soul. Bigots are so lacking in understanding, so narrow of mind, that they are blind to the realization that these very differences are the very heart of the diversity that makes humankind so special.

Such diversity is a blessing, in my view, something to be celebrated rather than feared and despised. I think I would die of sheer stultification and boredom if I had to live exclusively among people who were mere carbon copies of myself. Mercy, what a horribly depressing thought. I can barely live with myself at times. And pity my poor wife.

For those who might choose not to associate with the Verdants when they arrive simply because they are different, that will be their loss, and I pity them. As for me, I look forward with great anticipation, excitement, and enthusiasm to once again enjoy the stimulating company of these wonderful creatures, but this time on a more permanent basis.

I think it's going to be marvelous.

Anyone visiting the Third Street promenade of Santa Monica, near Los Angeles, will experience a multicultural adventure in a polyglot setting. It is a marketplace of variety where gay and straight couples of diverse racial and ethnic backgrounds mingle freely and effortlessly in an atmosphere of tolerance. It is a microcosm of what the world will be like someday. To view it is like peering into a diorama of the future.

My heart beats with excitement when I think how much more enriched this worldly melting pot will become with the addition of Verdant tourist couples strolling among the humans, all going about the business of enjoying the day.

The Verdants themselves, of course, have no illusions about the extent and depth of the various forms of prejudice and bigotry that exists in the human condition. But they do not intervene in the home-planet business of any species and certainly would not be so presumptuous as to tell humans how to run their own affairs.

All planets are sovereign. What we do on Earth is our business only. Only in space do the Verdants, and other members of the IFSP, insist on adherence to a specified code of conduct by all species. Humans will have to solve their own problems on their own soil. Only when those problems threaten to spill into space do the ETs get directly involved. And even then, they deal with the issues mostly in the cosmos, rarely on the home planet.

But the picture is not as bleak or gloomy as it might appear. The truth of the matter is, despite the widespread turmoil that tribal conflicts cause, the majority of humans have the capacity to transcend such petty hatreds.

The average person is basically good at heart and redeemable, I was told on several occasions. Otherwise, the Verdants would not be making such elaborate preparations for contact with Earth.

The News Business and the ET Presence

Pick up your daily newspaper and you'll find—besides news—just about something for everyone, ranging from horoscopes to editorials, comics to crossword puzzles. But one thing you're not likely to find is a reasoned, objective, balanced news story or feature article on the ET presence, as evidenced in the myriad of sightings of UFOs or the phenomenon of alien abductions. This is true for mainstream newspapers and magazines across the board, despite the fact that the empirical data suggest that interest in UFOs has never been greater nor has the level of UFO activity worldwide been more pronounced.

For decades, the mainstream press has virtually ignored the UFO community and the events that drive it. On those rare occasions when the subject does get coverage, the tenor of the stories is usually hostile, derisive, supercilious or even farcical. And even where sober news stories are written, rarely if ever are resources set aside for critical and in-depth reporting.

For instance, UFO web sites were reviewed in a column that appeared in the Business section of the *Los Angeles Times* on Thursday, September 14, 2000.

The headline?

"Spaced Cadets."

Well, it doesn't take a college degree in journalism or even a crude road map to know where this article is going. The columnist lists about a dozen sites while injecting the obligatory cutesy witticisms designed to exploit the "giggle factor" and titillate readers.

Like everyone else, reporters have their biases, but by and large I think most of those on the major metropolitan dailies across the land are reasonably successful in preventing those biases from creeping into their stories. But that dutiful vigilance does not seem to apply to UFO phenomena, an area in which the mainstream media seem to believe it is always open season. I can't think of a single other topic covered by the mainstream press—political, racial, ethnic, religious, economic, lifestyle, etc.—that is subject to the same level of unbalanced reporting and mocking commentary (on those rare occasions when coverage of the UFO field does occur). The very few exceptions to this only prove the rule.

To the layman, this attitude may be mystifying and begs the question: Why? Why do the mainstream media virtually ignore a growing database of information that strongly suggests the possibility of extraterrestrial activity? Why do they feel free—nay, even obligated—to mock and ridicule the very concept itself and besmirch respectable individuals who are engaged in responsible and legitimate inquiry? While I personally have reservations about such a viewpoint, nevertheless neither can I ignore the fact that many credentialed and responsible researchers believe that conspiratorial forces are at work behind the scenes. Others take a more charitable view by claiming that this neglect and derision demonstrate at the least an uninformed bias.

I raise these issues as one who has been on both sides of this divide; for years as a member of the mainstream press, and now—believe it or not—as an abductee with a story to tell. And while I'm intrigued by the claims of a government conspiracy, in truth I believe that the reason for the bias is not all that complicated once the dynamics of the forces at work are understood.

The Blame Must Be Shared

In tracking down the problem, one of the first places to look is the UFO community itself. As unfair as the coverage—however skimpy—has been in the mainstream press, part of the blame must be borne by UFO adherents themselves. A good example of this is that same *L.A. Times* column listing UFO web sites. On the one hand, the writers are somewhat justified in making sport because the sites they happened to list are pretty flaky. One, for example, sells a UFO detector that promises to alert the owner to the presence of any alien spacecraft within a 75-mile radius. The columnist points out: "That should give you plenty of time to put on your protective aluminum foil pyramid hat."

It's hard to fault the writer for skewering such a claim; the site probably begs for ridicule.

And yet, one has to wonder if the columnist began his search with a mindset to find the most outrageous sites and to ignore the ones dedicated to legitimate and careful inquiry. How many of the several hundred UFO-related sites did he actually visit before choosing the dozen or so that were listed?

Of course, every cause draws hitchhikers, and the UFO community will continue to pay the price for the embarrassing excesses of those unstable individuals who have attached themselves to the larger, responsible group. In addition, the UFO community must take responsibility for the fact that its own researchers are notorious for internecine quibbling and career rivalries.

But at the same time, I am largely impressed by the UFO community: When I took my first intimate and unbiased look into the field, I was surprised to discover that it's composed primarily of intelligent, rational, reasonable, educated people, many of whom have postgraduate degrees and have distinguished themselves in their professional fields.

Unfortunately, this larger group will begin to be taken more seriously only when it finds a way to dissociate itself from the flakes, the quibblers, the turf-builders, and the unbalanced and irrational minority. That's easier said than done, but several new initiatives launched by leaders in the UFO field may begin to do just that.

Justified Criticism of the Media

Now, let's turn our microscope on the media. Let me first make it clear that, on the whole, American mainstream newspapers do a fairly decent job of informing their readers while maintaining high standards of truth, accuracy, and fairness. I have always felt that to be the case, and still do. To maintain these high standards, journalists must approach unusual stories with a healthy dose of skepticism; in fact it's almost a requirement for meeting the goal of serving the public interest. But sometimes that skepticism can evolve into a blind spot—and the UFO/alien-abduction field is surely one of those cases. Obviously, I didn't think this was the case at first; it took my own personal abduction experience to discard my blinders and cause me to reassess the way the mainstream press has treated this phenomenon.

Admittedly, when the first major UFO reports burst

onto the scene some 50 years ago, the mainstream press covered them pretty extensively. The big story, of course, was the reported crash of an alien craft on a ranch near the town of Roswell, New Mexico, in 1947. It was a story that could hardly be ignored because high-level officials, both civilian and military, assumed prominent roles as the story played out. Without that level of involvement, though—which imbued it with an aura of respectability that had worldwide implications—the story might have gotten notice in a few community newspapers and then been quickly discarded and forgotten.

Meanwhile, important and well-reported stories followed upon Roswell on into the 1950s—for example, the extensive sightings by military and civilian witnesses over Washington, D.C., in 1952.

But as the years went by, the stories and reports began to get less and less coverage. Eventually, by sometime in the 1960s, the numerous reports of sightings worldwide became virtually ignored in the U.S. media.

To what can we attribute this? The primary problem at first was the lack of hard evidence available to the press. As numerous commentators have pointed out, any hard evidence that may have been recovered by the government was never released to the press—for obvious security reasons—throughout the Cold War era. Any such disclosures might have dangerously tipped the balance of the arms race, it has been claimed.

Occasionally, a reputable source such as an airline crew would report an encounter with a UFO. But for the most part, stories of abductions and sightings were being told by ordinary people, often living in remote areas, and these usually lacked corroborating witnesses or hard evidence to authenticate their tales.

Ignoring the phenomenon thus became an entrenched habit in the press, even as the situation changed after the end of the Cold War. Considerable anecdotal evidence has not only accumulated over a 50-year period, but the quality and quantity of the evidence of ET contact has improved. It is as if the ET presence itself has become factually more of a reality.

For example, in response to what appears to be an epidemic of reports of alien abductions in the last two decades, the chairman of the psychiatry department at Harvard, John Mack, stepped forward at considerable risk to his own career to provide substantive documentation of the phenomenon based on his own original research, and has written extensively and insightfully about it. UFO abduction reports have now become so commonplace that there is now a nationwide association of therapists, led by Dr. Leo Sprinkle, who meet regularly to discuss strategies for working with "experiencers."

In addition, among the many sightings in recent years were the spectacular scenes of mile-wide, low-flying triangular craft seen over Phoenix in 1997, witnessed by thousands and well photographed. And around the same time, Colonel Philip J. Corso (Ret.), a member of President Eisenhower's National Security Council and former head of the Foreign Technology Desk at the U.S. Army's Research & Development, came forward to reveal his perspective and interpretation of the facts around the Roswell incident, just a few years before his death. And in 1999 the French military released the so-called COMETA Report, explicitly endorsing the extraterrestrial hypothesis.

But none of these stories have received sufficient mainstream coverage. For example, I am told that the only daily newspaper in the country to cover the COMETA Report at the time the report was released was the *Boston Globe*.

Understandably, there is widespread belief in the UFO community that many reports of encounters known only to the government are being suppressed. These activists—who include prominent and respected scholars, investigators, and researchers—cite among other forms of evidence, documents uncovered under the Freedom of Information Act to support their contention that the government will go to extreme lengths to cover up the evidence. And greater disclosures are in store: As we go to press, one of the world's foremost UFO researchers, Dr. Steven Greer, is reportedly preparing to release unprecedented testimony from insiders in the government and the military. This disclosure includes more than 100 witnesses who have already been videotaped by his organization.

Nevertheless, in newsrooms across the country, hard-boiled reporters and editors continue to adopt a disdainful mindset in which they automatically characterize the people who report UFOs and abduction "events" as, to put it charitably, unreliable.

Even back in 1963 when I got into the business, there were probably very few journalists who didn't consider such reports the result of overactive imaginations by a variety of characters whose judgment was questionable. It got to the point where a reporter's judgment and credibility could come into question if he even so much as suggested to an editor that he wanted to cover one of these outrageous stories. Such a proposal could even jeopardize a career. The same caution applied to any editor who seriously considered assigning a reporter to cover the field.

One would think the pursuit of such a story must rank higher in importance than that of the alleged Loch Ness monster, which I'm sure has received much more ink over the years. Even if the monster was determined to be authentic—"Ancient Living Life Form Discovered!"—such a discovery would pale in significance when compared to a story of the detection of intelligent alien life.

But the reality is clear: For whatever reason, the peer pressures on reporters to not be identified with such stories became vise-like. I myself shared the majority view, but because I wasn't in a position to either assign or report stories, I personally didn't suffer the same pressures as those with whom I worked. Only after I had left the *Times* and had my own experience did I feel the full effects of the mocking attitudes that I myself so willingly embraced and inflicted. Talk about being hoisted on one's own petard!

In summary: There once were good and solid reasons for not covering UFO stories and reports in the early stages when there were only a handful, and when hard evidence simply wasn't available to reporters. The media are accountable to their readers and audiences, and as such they have to ensure that any story they report has at least a modicum of veracity and legitimacy. As a journalist, I not only understand this policy, I support it. A good reporter requires corroboration before he goes public with any story. The mainstream news media cannot be expected to run tales of abduction—or any other fantastic story, for that matter—simply by taking the word of someone who claims to have been so victimized. But the UFO story has taken on new dimensions since those early years. This current situation represents a fundamental change in the nature of the story. No longer is this phenomenon merely about random sightings, occasional abductions in rural areas, and speculations about government knowledge of the phenomenon; it is about huge numbers of very credible people coming forth with testimony about remarkable and extraordinary experiences. Based on journalism as I was taught it, understand it, and practiced it for three decades, just the names of the many high-profile individuals involved provide justification enough for legitimate treatment by the news community.

Phone Tips From Readers

Once again, to be fair, I should tell you that newspapers are deluged by reports from people relating fantastic stories of personal adventures for which there is no evidence. Many come from the unstable and unreliable at any time of the day, but the phone activity picks up as the day grows late and the level of alcohol consumption rises.

The *L.A. Times* actually has a "nut phone" manned by copy messengers, low-level editorial employees. *Times* editors on the city desk are actually quite good at determining within three or four sentences whether the person on the other end of the line is a legitimate news source or someone who has tipped one too many, is wrestling with his own personal demons, or is just a garden variety crank. If the caller is determined to be less than credible, the editor transfers the call to the nut phone.

The copy messenger's job is just to listen, to mollify if

possible, until the caller runs out of steam, at which time the "reporter" promises to look into the story, and the call is terminated.

Again, I saw nothing wrong with this practice while I was working in the newsroom.

However, from my new perspective I have now come to the realization that legitimate calls from ordinary people who have had abduction experiences or sightings of UFOs are routinely routed to the nut phone as well, and that is unfortunate.

That is where the blind spot comes into play, and I hadn't been able to see this until after my own abduction experience.

Random phone tips from readers rarely make news; big stories make news, and it usually takes important names—or big numbers—to make big stories.

The simplest rule is: The bigger the name, the bigger the news story. Obviously, if you get the flu, or I get the flu—or even if one of us gets abducted by alien beings—don't expect to see a story about it in the morning paper, unless you are an extremely prominent person.

Now if the president of the United States or perhaps the Pope is laid up for a few days with the flu, that might become a minor news story of two or three lines on one of the inside pages.

However, if a flu epidemic swept the country and millions of people were affected, that would be a legitimate news story—and a likely candidate for Page 1 coverage—by virtue of the sheer numbers of people afflicted. Most likely it would be a medical story and the mainstream press certainly would cover it.

If a prominent person—say the president of a major university or corporation—went public with a personal account of a UFO sighting or an alien abduction experience, there is no doubt that the story would be published because the name itself would be enough to justify a news story. Former President Jimmy Carter is a good case in point because the mainstream press covered the story prominently when he made it clear, as Chief Executive, that he had once witnessed a UFO.

Here is where I believe the mainstream press wears its blinders. If 1,000 or 10,000 or a million people report abduction experiences, that is a legitimate news story by virtue of the vast numbers of people making such reports. It deserves to be covered even if it turns out that the reports are nothing but the result of mass delusions, which in itself would be an important medical story. And as I have stated, bigger and bigger names are also coming into prominence in the UFO field. And finally, when the Verdants and the Ambassadors decide to go public as described in this book—well, that will be one the biggest stories of all.

Newsroom Dynamics

In order to understand why some stories are covered and others are virtually ignored, it is necessary to get a sense of the operational forces that drive these decisions. Small newspapers, whether they are weeklies, semi-weeklies, or dailies, are the training ground for reporters and editors. They are great places to learn the news business and to hone skills. Staff members not only get a chance to work in all areas of the operation, it is a practical necessity that they do so.

Reporters may find themselves covering a variety of beats—schools, police, government—as well as covering breaking news—fires, accidents—taking photographs, and perhaps even writing a column. They may find themselves pressed into service to lay out pages, edit copy and write headlines, and oversee the makeup of the pages in the composing room.

I performed all of those chores, and more, when I worked on my first newspaper, a 32,000-circulation semi-weekly. Even when I was just a reporter, I wrote an occasional editorial when the editor was hard-pressed for time as the ever-present deadlines neared.

On major metropolitan dailies, with their larger staffs, reporters and editors perform more specialized duties and rarely are required, or even get the opportunity, to take on tasks outside of their assigned duties.

There is very little, if any, crossover between assigned duties. Many reporters are assigned particular beats, and they typically become specialists in those areas whereas reporters on smaller papers are more often generalists.

It is the beat reporters' responsibility to stay abreast of major developments in their particular fields. Rather than relying upon an editor to assign them stories on their beats, it is actually their duty to keep the editors informed about events that will become the basis of forthcoming stories.

Other reporters are general assignment writers who cover no particular beat but are available on a moment's notice to cover any story dealt to them. It could be as important as a fast-breaking news story involving a barricaded gunman with hostages or as soft as a feature story on a cuddly new addition to the city zoo.

So what does all of this have to do with the UFO/alien-abduction community?

I believe it gives yet another explanation why the American mainstream press has failed to adequately cover a momentous phenomenon that would have generated stories on a worldwide scale if it were occurring in any other more orthodox field, such as politics or religion. Television, I might add, has been much more in the forefront on this story, particularly the cable channels that rely heavily upon documentaries. Again, the so-called traditional, or family-hour stations, have been almost as quiet on the subject as has the mainstream press.

I do not know personally of any major newspaper that has assigned a beat reporter to cover developments in the UFO/alien-abduction field. There could be a couple, but I am not aware of them. Some papers have given some guarded coverage to the field, but the stories are more about personalities in the field in the form of feature stories. Others have more to do with routine coverage of community events.

However, as far as I am aware, there is no concentrated effort, no commitment of major resources by any conventional newspaper to investigate the UFO phenomenon in depth to try to find out what is really going on.

It is important that contactees, enthusiasts, activists, and investigators face this reality.

And even if there were a reporter or an editor who believed that a story lay lurking behind the phenomenon—and I didn't personally know anyone who was—the pressure to keep such thoughts to oneself were and are enormous.

As such, what assignment editor who cared about his career, about climbing the corporate ladder, would have the temerity to commit the necessary resources of the newspaper required and designate a reporter to go out into the field and investigate the phenomenon? The assignment could take months, possibly years, and the costs would be tremendous.

Can you visualize the looks that the editor could get from the skeptical reporter? Can you imagine the complaint that the reporter might take to a higher editorial authority? Can you picture the position the assignment editor would be in when called on the carpet to explain his "bizarre" decision?

Then you can understand another reason why the story is not being adequately covered. The sad result is that one of the greatest stories of our time, ironically, is one of the most underreported or our time.

Will the story ever be covered? I personally think it will.

When? Certainly after the extraterrestrials make official contact with government leaders and the story breaks worldwide. Of course, then it will be far too late as far as the mission of journalism to be ahead of the news.

Coverage could happen before that, but it's going to require some fortuitous circumstances. Here's my speculative version of how that might unfold:

Someday, somewhere, a visionary editor on a mainstream newspaper is going to be promoted into a position of sufficient authority, and is going to look at the phenomenon more closely, more objectively. She is going to admit to herself that the prodigious numbers of people reporting alien-abductions is in itself enough of a reason to justify an investigation. She will finally accept that all of these people can no longer be dismissed as unreliable or unstable—"nuts," in newsroom terminology. Her journalistic instincts will tell her that this is a legitimate news story that has been ignored too long and that the American people deserve to be informed.

And then she is going to display some uncommon courage—which is doubtless going to cause a storm of controversy in the newsroom—and boldly commit resources, both money and people, with the directive to go out there and get the story.

"Find out what's going on," she will bark. "I don't care if it takes a year. I want to know if there are aliens in the neighborhood or if thousands of people worldwide are suffering mass delusions. I want you to pore over government documents. I want you to go after any evidence that may have been suppressed all these years. Then, and only then, will I be satisfied."

A Crack in the Wall

In my own case, I have personally witnessed a small crack in the wall of resistance. Nothing major, just a small fissure. In October 1998, I was among several people interviewed by a reporter for a local independent Los Angeles television station. His editor had seen a report that had come out several months earlier in which a respected group of scientists—led by Prof. Peter A. Sturrock of Stanford University—suggested that perhaps the time had come for the scientific community to start taking a serious look at the UFO phenomenon.

This in itself was a groundbreaking event that the mainstream media did report (though I didn't notice any rush by journalists to follow up on the Stanford professor's suggestion themselves). In any case, the editor at the TV station bucked the traditional policy of keeping UFO stories at arm's length and assigned a reporter to do a serious piece on the subject. It was an act of exemplary editorial courage.

This turned out to be the first exposure of my story in the mainstream media. Previous to this, it was being covered only within the UFO and New Age communities. The crack widened a bit again in the summer of 2000 when I was in Phoenix to do a videotaped interview for a private documentary project. A local Fox Network TV news crew showed up and did an interview, portions of which appeared that same day. In addition, the station scheduled me for another interview for its morning show the next day. I saw both segments back in my hotel room and was pleasantly surprised that they played the story straight—not a smirk in sight. The complete interview, incidentally, was aired in a special report some months later.

However, I am not so naive as to believe that there will be a great rush in the newsroom to start covering the phenomenon seriously. It is obvious that attitudes in the media are still too rigid, biases run too deep, and peer pressure and management pressure to steer clear of the subject still too intense for that to occur overnight. Formidable obstacles still have to be overcome before journalists approach the story thoughtfully. In the meantime, it's still *de rigueur* within the industry to look down the nose at such reports.

I was certain as I was writing my first book that I would face serious problems with the mainstream press—assuming that I was not totally ignored by them—but I made a determined decision to publish that book, and the book you hold in your hands, because I believe I have something important to say. If I have succeeded in shedding some light on this murky, chaotic subject; if I have planted seeds among the mainstream media that might someday lead to more open coverage of this phenomenon; and, if I have encouraged a few biased individuals in the media to open their minds and rethink their positions—then the difficulties will have been well worth it.

Receive News and Updates on the Contact

For regular updates and breaking news on the Verdant-human contact project, or to get in touch with Phillip Krapf, please go to:

TheChallengeofContact.com

You may also order both of Phillip Krapf's books at this website.

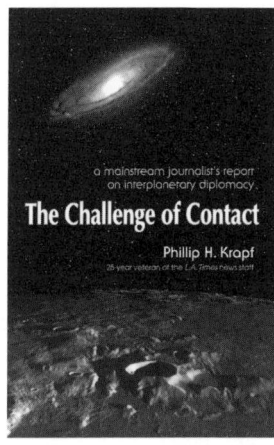

Give the gift of
The Challenge of Contact
to your friends

☐ YES, I want _____ copies of **The Challenge of Contact** at $19.95 each — please include $4.50 shipping for the first book and $1.00 for each additional book. California residents add 7.25% sales tax.

Name _____

Company _____

City _____ State _____ Zip _____

Phone _____

Email _____

Total _____

☐ Check or money order   ☐ Visa   ☐ Mastercard

Card # _____ Exp. _____

Signature _____

Call our Toll Free order line: 1.888.267.4446
Fax your order to: 415.898.1434
Order online: TheChallengeofContact.com

Please make your check payable and return to:

Origin Press
1122 Grant Avenue, Suite C
Novato, CA 94945

Timothy Wyllie's
Adventures Among Spiritual Intelligences
Angels, Aliens, Dolphins & Shamans

The new sequel to the classic *Dolphins, ETs and Angels*

☐ YES, I want _____ copies of **Adventures Among Spiritual Intelligences** at $16.95 each — please include $4.50 shipping for the first book and $1.00 for each additional book. CA residents add 7.25% sales tax.

Name _____

Company _____

City _____ State _____ Zip _____

Phone _____

Email _____

Total _____

☐ Check or money order ☐ Visa ☐ Mastercard

Card # _____ Exp. _____

Signature _____

Call our Toll Free order line: 1.888.267.4446
Fax your order to: 415.898.1434
Order online: www.ikosmos.com/WisdomEditions

Please make your check payable and return to:

Wisdom Editions
1122 Grant Avenue, Suite C
Novato, CA 94945